NATURAL RESOURCES AND ENERGY:
Theory and Policy

NATURAL RESOURCES AND ENERGY:
Theory and Policy

by
Chennat Gopalakrishnan

ANN ARBOR SCIENCE
PUBLISHERS INC / THE BUTTERWORTH GROUP

PREFACE

Natural resources and energy are rapidly gaining importance as areas of serious academic inquiry. This growing scholarly concern is largely the result of increasingly critical natural resource scarcities and energy shortages that pose a serious threat to sustained economic growth and improved quality of life. The significantly heightened interest in the field is beginning to manifest itself in the form of in-depth critical scrutinies and analyses of a number of specific problems and issues. This represents a distinct departure from the earlier efforts, which were largely in the nature of surveys and overviews of broad problem areas.

This book consists of theoretical discussions and case studies of some key issues of current and continuing interest in the natural resources and energy field. The topics studied include such frontier issues as the economics of water transfer, the role of multinational corporations in ocean resource development, methodological issues in estimating energy requirements, institutional constraints to water resource development and coastal zone management, biomass as an alternative energy source, and the role of natural resources in economic development. The book attempts to synthesize theoretical insights and empirical research findings to provide an integrated macro-framework from which to examine and analyze a variety of natural resource problems. The material is so organized as to illustrate and illuminate the application of theory to the solution of real-world problems.

The book examines natural resource and energy problems in the local, national and international contexts. A special feature of the book is its detailed discussion of the "institutional"—political, legal, social and cultural—aspects of natural resource allocation and policy. The author's approach is interdisciplinary and eclectic, and it is not intended to advocate or endorse any particular philosophy or ideology.

This book is primarily designed as a supplementary or companion volume to a textbook in natural resource, water, marine or energy economics and policy at the advanced undergraduate or graduate level. Several of the topics discussed in the book have been class-tested and found to be of considerable interest to the students. Although the book is directed mainly to an academic audience, it could prove to be of interest to a much larger constituency consisting of policy analysts, administrators, planners and researchers.

Chennat Gopalakrishnan

ACKNOWLEDGMENTS

The author is grateful to the following publishers for granting permission to reprint the papers listed below:

Chapter 1, "The Economics of Water Transfer," from *The American Journal of Economics and Sociology* 32(4):395-403 (1973).

Chapter 2, "The Doctrine of Prior Appropriation and Its Impact on Water Development: A Critical Survey," from *The American Journal of Economics and Sociology* 32(1):61-72 (1973).

Chapter 3, "Multinational Corporations, Nation-States and Ocean Resource Management: The Impact of a 200-Mile Economic Zone," from *The American Journal of Economics and Sociology* 38(3):253-260 (1979).

Chapter 4, "Estimating Energy Requirements for Agriculture: Some Methodological Issues," from *Resource Management and Optimization* 1(2):197-209 (1980).

Chapter 5, "Water Resource Development: Some Institutional Aspects: A Case History of Montana," from *The American Journal of Economics and Sociology* 30(4):421-428 (1971).

Chapter 6, "Economic Growth Through Water Resource Development: India," from *Water Resources Bulletin* (American Water Resources Association) Paper No. 72041, 8(3):459-472 (1972).

Chapter 7, "Some Institutional Constraints to Coastal Zone Management: A Case Study of Hawaii," from *The American Journal of Economics and Sociology* 33(3):225-232 (1974).

Chapter 8, "Coastal Zone Use Conflicts and Their Identification: The Use of Compatibility Matrixes," from the *Proceedings of Marine Technology Society* (September 1976) pp. 27 C-1-5.

Chapter 9, "Economic Potential of Bagasse as an Alternative Energy Source: The Hawaiian Experience," from *Agriculture and Energy* (New York: Academic Press, Inc., 1977), pp. 479-488.

The author wishes to express his special thanks to the following individuals for their unfailing encouragement and support to his creative and intellectual endeavors: Harold L. Baker, Jack R. Davidson, Frank S. Scott, Jr. and Heinz Spielmann, colleagues; Jagdish P. Bhati, Ibrahim E. Dik and Prahlad Kasturi, graduate students in the Department of Agricultural and Resource Economics, University of Hawaii; John L. Fischer, Dean, Faculty of Agricultural and Food Sciences, American University of Beirut; Helmer C. Holje, Professor of Resource Economics, Montana State University.

Chennat Gopalakrishnan is Professor of Agricultural and Resource Economics, College of Tropical Agriculture and Human Resources, University of Hawaii. He earned his PhD in Agricultural Economics at Montana State University, and his MS and BS in Economics from Kerala University, India.

Dr. Gopalakrishnan's research has been primarily in natural resource economics, particularly in energy, marine resources and water resources. The focus of one of his current research projects is the evaluation of alternative governmental policies affecting energy use and availability in agriculture. The primary objective of another project is the study of economic, institutional and environmental factors that will facilitate decisions on the utilization of geothermal energy by prospective users.

Dr. Gopalakrishnan served on the research staff of the National Council of Applied Economic Research, New Delhi, where he worked on projects dealing with various aspects of India's economic development, and also was a senior researcher for the *Economic Times*, Bombay.

Dr. Gopalakrishnan is listed in International Who's Who in Education, American Men and Women of Science and Who's Who in the West. He has published extensively in professional journals as well as presented papers at major conferences. He received the 1980 Gamma Sigma Delta Award for outstanding researcher in recognition of his research and writings in energy economics and policy.

TO
MALINI AND SHALINI

CONTENTS

Introduction 1

Part 1
Theoretical Perspectives

1. The Economics of Water Transfer 11

   Introduction 11
   Water Transfer and Economic Development 12
   Allocation of Water Among Competing Uses. 16
   Water Transfer: Efficiency vs Equity. 20

2. The Doctrine of Prior Appropriation and Its Impact
   on Water Development: A Critical Study 23

   Introduction 23
   Background. 24
   Doctrine of Prior Appropriation: Theory 25
   Prior Appropriation in the Western States: Practice 27
   Conclusions. 37

3. Multinational Corporations, Nation-States and
   Ocean Resource Management: The Impact of a
   200-Mile Economic Zone 39

   Introduction 39
   Impact of Extended Jurisdiction. 40
   MNC and Nation-States: Partners in Development 41

Alternative Futures of World Order: A Third Dimension 46
Conclusions. 47

4. Estimating Energy Requirements for Agriculture:
    Some Methodological Issues 49

    Introduction 49
    Energy Requirement Estimation. 50
    Energy Flow Model for Agriculture. 51
    Economic Energy 53
    Dimensions of Energy Studies. 54
    Conclusions. 61

Part 2
Case Studies

5. Water Resource Development: Some Institutional
    Aspects: A Case History of Montana. 65

    Introduction 65
    The Legal Framework 66
    Conservancy Districts 68
    Role of State Agencies 70
    Role of Federal Government. 71
    Conservation vs Dam Building. 72
    Conclusions. 74

6. Economic Growth Through Water Resource
    Development: India. 75

    Introduction 75
    Developing India's Water Resources: Objectives 76
    Impact of Water Development on Indian Economy. 77
    Role of Water in the "Green Revolution" 85
    Employment Potential 86
    India's Water Planning: A Critical Appraisal 89
    Institutional Constraints 92
    Conclusions. 97

7. Some Institutional Constraints to Coastal Zone
   Management: A Case Study of Hawaii. 101

   Introduction 101
   Shoreline Ownership: Oligopoly in Action 102
   Conflict of Interests: The Swing of the Pendulum. 104
   Jurisdictional Overlapping: The Shadowy Landscape . . .107
   Public Interest: The Forgotten Dimension 108
   Conclusions. 110

8. Coastal Zone Use Conflicts and Their Identification:
   The Use of Compatibility Matrixes 113

   Introduction 113
   Shoreline Development and Use Conflicts. 114
   Impact on Public Interest 116
   Identifying Use Conflicts: The Use of Compatibility
   Matrixes 118

9. Economic Potential of Bagasse as an Alternative
   Energy Source: The Hawaiian Experience. 123

   Introduction 123
   Institutional Setting 124
   Bagasse as an Energy Source .126
   The Hawaiian Experience 129
   Optimizing Bagasse Use. 131
   Conclusions. 133

Index. 135

INTRODUCTION

The role of natural resources and energy in the context of economic growth, both at the micro and macro levels, has recently begun to engage the serious attention of scholars, policymakers, planners and even laymen. This resurgence of interest in a vital, although heretofore somewhat neglected, area is largely the upshot of the increasingly critical energy shortages and natural resource scarcities which pose a serious threat to continued economic growth at an undiminished pace. One of the more important spinoffs of the scholarly concern with natural resources and energy is the identification and delineation of specific issues and problems for in-depth critical scrutiny—something that had not been attempted until recently in any sustained fashion, except for random studies undertaken by an occasional interested scholar.

This book is a modest attempt to fill this gap. The nine chapters represent a synthesis of theoretical insights and empirical research on some frontier issues in the natural resources and energy field. The problems examined are wide-ranging in scope and diversity and are of compelling interest because of their relevance and topicality. It should also be noted that despite their importance, very few attempts have been made in the past to explore the topics discussed in this book in terms of theory as well as practice. In that sense, this book represents an original contribution to a rapidly growing field of increasing importance.

The book is divided into two parts. The four chapters in Part 1 provide theoretical perspectives on some key issues of current and continuing importance in the natural resources field, specifically water resources, ocean resources and energy. Part 2 consists largely of case studies or case histories, designed to illustrate and illuminate the theoretical perspectives developed in Part 1. Together, the chapters constitute a coherent whole in that they provide a holistic macroframework from which to view the issues discussed in terms of their theoretical import as well as their operational viability.

Chapter 1, "The Economics of Water Transfer," discusses the economic implications of transferring water from low-yielding, conventional uses (mainly agricultural) to newly emerging and more productive uses (recreational and industrial) to enhance the value and productivity of water. The limited supply of water in relation to the rapidly growing demand for it makes this type of transfer almost imperative for the optimum use of water resources. The chapter presents evidence which clearly shows that reallocation of water from agricultural to industrial, municipal and recreational uses is capable of markedly expanding the development potential of water-deficient regions.

The strategic role of water in the development of the semi-arid and arid regions is nowhere more manifest than in the legal doctrines governing its development and use. Chapter 2 attempts to examine critically the legal framework encompassing water resource development in the western United States. The analysis deals with surface and groundwater laws separately, and presents supportive evidence to the conclusion that the doctrine of prior appropriation has through the years evolved into a fairly dynamic body of laws whose operational efficiency has increased considerably in the context of the rapidly expanding water needs of the western United States.

Chapters 5 and 6 provide case studies designed to illustrate some of the salient points developed above. These explore the institutional dimensions of water resource development in a national as well as an international context. Both chapters focus attention on some of the institutional impediments to water resource development and point out how these constraints have considerably slowed down the optimum development of water resources in the cases studied—Montana and India.

Chapter 5, "Water Resource Development: Some Institutional Aspects—A Case History of Montana," shows that the success of a program of water resource development depends not merely on economic considerations, but on a host of institutional factors as well. The search for efficiency in water utilization through water transfer can be successful only if these institutional aspects are reckoned with. To overcome most of the major institutional blocks, in addition to removing the legal and administrative handicaps, concerted efforts should be undertaken to educate people at the "grass roots" level.

Chapter 6, "Economic Growth through Water Resource Development: India," studies the impact of India's multidimensional water development programs on the pace and pattern of its economic growth. The chapter analyzes in detail the impact of India's massive water programs on the country's economy in terms of a number of indices of economic growth. Despite its pronounced impact on the economy, India's water-planning strategy is shown to have some glaring weaknesses: the failure to incorporate "indirect benefits" in cost-benefit calculations, the underuse of water potential and the progressive increase in the cost of irrigating each acre of land. The chapter concludes that the prevailing institutional structure in India constitutes a major deterrent to the diffusion of the benefits of water development. There are stubborn psychological factors which make the adoption of innovative irrigation practices difficult. Thus, there is an overwhelming need to revamp India's institutional framework.

Three chapters in the book are devoted to the study of ocean resources. Chapter 3, on "Multinational Corporations, Nation-States and Ocean Resource Management," addresses a theme of considerable relevance to the future development of ocean resources. It studies the potential impact of a 200-mile exclusive economic zone on the interrelationship between nation-states and multinational corporations.

One of the startling conclusions presented on the basis of empirical evidence in Chapter 3 is that the extension of coastal state jurisdiction to 200 nautical miles would lead to a unique stituation in the ownership of ocean resources: 15 coastal states would receive among them approximately 42% of the world's 200-mile economic zone area. At least eight of these countries are less-developed coastal states (LDCS) which lack the key factors, capital, technology and managerial skill necessary to tap these resources. As a result, the reliance of the LDCS on marine multinational corporations (MNC) will markedly increase because a significant part of marine technology exists in the private sector. Concurrently, a dramatic rise in the control of coastal states over MNC engaged in ocean resource development will occur. The chapter develops the challenging thesis that under the new regime of ocean resource management, the relationship between MNC and nation-states is likely to be one of constructive partnership in development, rather than one of conflict and discord.

Chapters 7 and 8 view the problem of ocean resource management from a different perspective. Both chapters attempt to look at the complex range of problems associated with the management of the vital coastal zone or shoreline resources in terms of an overwhelmingly marine state: Hawaii.

Chapter 7 examines critically the factors which impede the formulation and implementation of an effective system for optimum management of Hawaii's vital shoreline. The problems plaguing Hawaii's coastal zone management are primarily the result of institutional factors, some of them rather unique. The chapter identifies these as:

1. the oligopolistic structure of the state's shoreline ownership;
2. continuing conflicts and controversies among an array of shoreline interests: the private owners, the environmental and conservation groups, and the government agencies;
3. jurisdictional overlapping and lack of interagency coordination; and
4. absence of effective institutional mechanisms to ascertain "public" interest and incorporate it in coastal zone legislation.

The chapter concludes that institutional factors, despite their overriding importance, have received scant attention in the formulation of Hawaii's coastal zone policy and urges for a revamping of its archaic institutional infrastructure.

Chapter 8, "Coastal Zone Use Conflicts and Their Identification," attempts to study some of Hawaii's coastal zone conflicts, examines their impact on public interest and suggests
the use of a technique for the identification of use conflicts.
The chapter identifies, describes and discusses a number of use
conflicts that have resulted from the development of Hawaii's
coastal zone for recreational (resort), urban and industrial
purposes. This is followed by an appraisal of the impact of these
conflicts on public needs and interest. The chapter concludes
with a discussion of "compatibility matrixes," and their application to conflict identification in the context of shoreline
development.

It is pointed out that the use of compatibility matrixes as
part of a resource capability analysis should aid coastal zone
planners considerably in allocating the scarce coastal zone
resources in an optimal fashion. These matrixes should serve as
much-needed guides or pointers to steer clear of potential use
conflicts and the consequent waste of precious resources.

There are two chapters on energy. Chapter 4, the last chapter
in Part 1, addresses a problem of crucial importance in the
estimation of energy requirements. The focus of the chapter is
on some methodological issues that are especially relevant in
accurately determining the energy needs of agriculture. The
chapter points out that there is at present a severe dearth of
reliable information on direct as well as indirect energy requirements of the different sectors of the agricultural economy.
This has made meaningful projections of future energy needs
for the different crops and livestock exceedingly difficult. The
chapter identifies and discusses some of the problems besetting
energy requirements estimation for agriculture and develops an
alternative approach embodied in an energy-flow model for
agriculture. It also identifies six dimensions—product determination, stages of production, energy source, levels of technology,
geographic areas and time—crucial to the determination of
energy needs, and examines their implications from a methodological perspective.

Chapter 9, the last chapter in the book, is a case study of a
successful effort in Hawaii to use biomass as an alternative

energy source, a topic that should be of compelling interest to energy researchers as well as policymakers. The chapter represents a first attempt to explore the economic potential of bagasse (the fibrous residue of sugarcane left after crushing and extraction of the juices) as an important source of energy for Hawaii. The chapter gives a brief description of the institutional setting of sugarcane; discusses the extent to which the use of bagasse as an energy source has progressed and estimates its potential generating capacity; proposes specific strategies to expand its supply; and assesses its environmental impact in the context of energy generation.

The chapter points out that Hawaiian sugar industry currently generates about 75% of its energy needs from processing bagasse, an especially noteworthy conclusion in light of the increasing recognition of biomass as a viable energy source. The study further concludes that the low environmental impact of bagasse compared to other potential energy sources is significant, thus holding out the promise of a readily available, relatively nonpolluting alternative energy source.

As is evident from the foregoing discussion, the book draws attention to some major themes which have special relevance in the context of natural resources and energy policy formulation. First and foremost, a sensible natural resources and energy policy simply cannot be predicated on purely economic considerations; a whole range of "institutional" factors—political, legal, social and cultural—have to be carefully woven into its fabric to forge an exquisite synthesis of all the relevant variables. Such an approach would ensure a proper balance and judicious blending of the diversity of interests that ought to be reckoned with in the formulation of a successful and effective policy.

Chapters 5 through 8 amply demonstrate how crucial such an approach is to develop realistic, viable, effective resource management policies in terms of specific resources, nationally as well as globally.

Second, the need to adapt and modify institutions and legal arrangements to meet changing and challenging societal needs is crucial to effective policy formulation. Stated differently, the natural resources policy should be flexible, dynamic, and always receptive to change. Chapter 2 on the doctrine of prior appropriation provides some insights into the dynamics of evolutionary change.

Third, the thesis is developed that natural resources constitute the common heritage of mankind and that both the private and the public sectors have a vital stake in their optimal management. Consequently, it is imperative to establish a dialogue between the two parties as a prelude to policy formulation, in light of broad but well-defined common goals. How this could be accomplished is shown in Chapter 3.

Finally, two key issues central to the formulation of a realistic energy policy are discussed and illustrated. Chapter 4 develops a strong case for methodological sophistication in estimating energy requirements, because imprecise estimates have made energy needs forecasting all too often an exercise in futility. Chapter 9 focuses attention on the potential and promise of alternative energy sources, renewable and relatively nonpolluting, in alleviating the nation's critical energy shortages. Thus, the book draws attention to the need to look at the problem of resource scarcity and availability from a methodologically sound and innovative perspective.

Part 1

THEORETICAL PERSPECTIVES

CHAPTER 1

THE ECONOMICS OF WATER TRANSFER

INTRODUCTION

An aspect of water resource development that currently generates a good deal of interest among economists relates to the "economics of water transfer." The "economics of water transfer" deals with the economic implications of transferring water from low-yielding, conventional uses (mainly agricultural) to newly emerging and more productive uses (industrial and recreational) to enhance the value and productivity of water. The limited supply of water in relation to the fast-expanding demand for it makes this type of transfer almost imperative for the optimum use of water resources.

This chapter is primarily an attempt to study the economic underpinnings of the allocation of water among competing uses. The impact of transferring water from low- to high-productive uses on the pace and pattern of economic development is examined in some detail. This is followed by a discussion of the economic implications of water transfer. The allocation of water in terms of the market for water rights is studied, and, the various ramifications involved in water pricing are identified. The final section views the problem of water transfer and its consequences from the standpoints of both efficiency and equity and highlights some of the relevant issues.

WATER TRANSFER AND ECONOMIC DEVELOPMENT

The use of water in the United States has been growing in recent years at a much faster pace than the growth in population. Consequently, in the historically water-scarce regions of the United States, the pattern of water allocation over the next several years is likely to set definite limitations on the nature of the region's economic growth and, hence, on the economic growth of the nation as a whole.

Planning and action to meet current and future needs for water and its services are primarily matters of public decision. In the West there is a further element of public participation. Here, under appropriation law, shares of the water supply are allocated to specific uses on a property-right basis, and these rigidities are, in turn, written into interstate compacts on water use. Thus, the "free market" is a limited instrument for determining the relative desirability of water's alternative use—more so than it is in the case of most other resource products [1].

In certain states, however, subject to administrative controls, water rights can be bought and sold. Hence, the market forces can help allocate water among competing uses.

It is necessary, therefore, to study the effects on the economy of the different patterns of water use, in light of the estimated increase in the growth of population and economic activity. An interdisciplinary approach involving economists, geologists, engineers, biologists and lawyers can be of much value in this connection. A pioneering effort in this direction is Wollman's study on *The Value of Water in Alternative Uses* [1]. This study describes eight possible patterns for the use of unappropriated water in the San Juan and Rio Grande river basins in New Mexico. The eight possible patterns of water use described in that book represent different combinations of water according to three major uses: municipal/industrial, recreational and agricultural. The results of the study indicated that the contribution of the Rio Grande basin to the gross national product (GNP) would be, per acre-foot, about $50 for irrigation, compared to $200–300 for fish and wildlife habitat and $3000–4000/ac-ft in industry. This result, however, does not warrant the assumption that because industry yielded the highest value-added per acre-foot of water, and hence constituted the highest productivity, all available water should be allotted to industry.

The same results were obtained by analyzing the basic data on municipal/industrial, agricultural and recreational uses of water in terms of variations in profit rates and in benefit-cost ratios. Thus, high-industry models yielded benefit-cost ratios of 6.0 and 4.7, whereas high-irrigation models gave ratios of 2.1 and 2.0 [1].

The principal indicators used in the Wollman study to estimate the value of water in alternative uses were:

1. gross product,
2. primary value added,
3. value added by purchase,
4. secondary value added,
5. water costs,
6. employment and population,
7. capital requirements and capital supply.

Economic development can continue at an undiminished pace only through a process that will allow complete or full use of available supplies of water and also enable easy and advantageous transfers to "high-value" or more productive uses as these emerge. Optimum economic growth can be accomplished only by making necessary adjustments to meet the ever-growing demands. For this to become a reality, the engineering and economic elements of a water resource program should provide maximum flexibility of water use to satisfy the rapidly changing optimum patterns of water demand.

Thus, it has been shown that reallocation of water from agricultural to industrial/municipal and recreational uses is capable of markedly expanding the development potential of water-deficient regions. This fact makes clear the importance of efficient mechanisms for the transfer of water from lower- to higher-value uses in these regions. Water has to be transferred smoothly to support industrial and urban growth in the West if the West is to continue to grow. In addition, as water supplies become more stringent, it becomes highly important that water used in agriculture is applied to the most productive lands and crops by the most efficient methods.

Renshaw [2] has estimated the mean value of water per acre-foot for different uses (Table I). These figures, although not applicable to all situations, still give us an idea of the comparative range of values.

The following specific examples indicate how a reallocation of water from one use to another could bring about a substantial change in the contribution of water to economic development. Criddle cites as an example the transfer of water from agricultural to industrial purposes by referring to a development of the Price River in Carbon County, UT [3]. It is pointed out that the direct and indirect returns from the agricultural use of water in this area would represent only a small fraction of the returns likely to be generated by the creation of an electric plant. He further states that the estimates of the total returns from industry in Carbon County amount to over $28 million/yr compared with the total agricultural returns of about $1.25 million/yr. Despite this, however, in this area about 3 ac-ft of water are used for irrigation for every acre-foot used for industrial and other uses.

Table I. Mean Value of Water per Acre Foot

Use	Value Per Acre-Foot ($)
Domestic	100.19
Industrial	40.73
Irrigation	1.67
Power	0.67
Waste Disposal	0.63
Inland Navigation	0.05
Commercial Fisheries	0.03

Another example relates to a somewhat similar development in Kemmerer, WY—a storage reservoir with 28,000 ac-ft capacity under construction on Ham's Fork River to supply water for a 300,000-Watt thermal plant [3]. It is estimated that the same amount of water used for agricultural purposes in this area would have a much smaller impact on the local economy compared to the effect of the industrial use of water.

The above two examples, however, have some serious limitations. For one thing, the comparison is between a consumptive use of water (irrigation) and a nonconsumptive use (industry) on the other. Second, the possibility for the creation of a multipurpose project which can use water for a number of purposes, including irrigation, is not explored in those examples. The possible total returns from the creation of a multipurpose project in each case could have been much higher than the returns from industrial use of water alone. Third, the figures employed by Criddle to estimate the possible returns from the industrial use of water are averages (or means) only. Thus, they are unable to indicate the marginal productivity of water in either industrial or agricultural use. Finally, a complete transfer of the available water from agriculture to industry in communities which are basically agricultural would tend to upset the familiar pattern of life and could result in a number of "social costs." Viewed in this perspective, any argument for a wholesale transfer of water from agriculture to industry loses much of its weight.

The transfer of water from less productive to more productive uses contributes to economic growth indirectly. The concept of "externalities" or "spillover effects" refers to these economic effects which lie outside the decision-making process of microunits of water users [4]. In the case of water transfer, these effects are generated by water supply and income interdependencies of a more general character in the water-using community. In the context of externalities, a water transfer is considered desirable if the new use after the transfer creates an increase in income. This is regarded as the major welfare criterion for analysis of the allocation problem and the role played by institutions in effecting such transfer. Externalities from changing water use have distinct welfare implications resulting from major changes in the pattern and pace of overall economic development.

There is a close relationship between water transfer and economic development. Consequently, it has become increasingly clear that the basic policy in water resource development is to achieve the most economic allocation of water to maximize the net benefits to society. How exactly could this optimal allocation of the limited water resources between competing uses be accomplished? It is here that the market mechanism and pricing policies assume a strategic role.

ALLOCATION OF WATER AMONG COMPETING USES

To understand the nature of the transfer of water among alternative uses, one must examine rather closely two separate aspects of the problem: (1) the market for water rights, and (2) the problem of pricing waters. These two aspects are closely interwoven, and they exert a significant influence on the allocation of water among a variety of competing uses.

The Market for Water Rights

The market mechanism with appropriate modifications could play an important role in the transfer of rights to water supplies. This is specifically true because the legal and administrative procedures and precedents surrounding the transfer of water rights are extremely cumbersome. Hence, it is believed that greater reliance on the market process of purchase and sale would lead to more productive use of water and greater economic returns.

This is a particularly important problem in much of the West, where efficient use of limited water supplies is important to regional economic advancement, and where water law tends to inhibit transfer out of low-value irrigation uses to high-value municipal and industrial uses [5].

As Kelso points out, if market forces are to be employed to allocate water among uses and users, water rights owners must be permitted to buy and sell their rights [6]. However, little is known about the market for water rights. How effective are such markets in allocating water to its "highest and best" use? Both Kelso and Brewer are of the opinion that the market for water rights deviates considerably from the textbook definition of a "free market." For instance, instead of a large number of buyers and sellers, there may be a small number or even a single buyer or seller.

Brewer maintains that in the context of a market, water transfer is often equated with a sales transaction [7]. The parties to the transfer may be individuals or agencies, and the process may occur at a wholesale level, a retail level or it may exist between different levels. Transfer between entities at the same marketing level may be termed "horizontal" transfers, as distinct from "vertical" transfers, which involve several market levels. Examples of the latter include transfers of water from a district to its members or from a federal or state agency to a local district.

Thus, producers and sellers of water are not numerically equivalent in the water market. Some producers sell water entirely on a wholesale basis. An instance in point is the sale of water by the Bureau of Reclamation through the Central Valley Project in California. Others are both wholesalers and retailers; local irrigation districts belong to this category. These examples clearly indicate the need to modify the conventional market approach in the case of water transfer.

The market mechanism has also other ramifications. There is, for example, the crucial question of how effectively the market exchange of property rights in water (the mechanism implied by the prior appropriation doctrine in the western United States) can result in economically optimal water allocation, especially, on a large scale. For one thing, the impact of water allocation on third parties (i.e., nonparticipants in the market-determined decision to transfer) has to be reckoned with. These third parties include the service community of an irrigation project, downstream users who depend upon return flows and down-

stream users affected by changes in the quality of flow atten-
dant to changes in use. Second, it is not yet evident that the
best method for water transfer in the arid West is the exchange
of water rights in markets, because of the difficulty in arriving at reasonably certain definitions of rights when major
third party effects that result from water quality deterioration
and return-flow dependency are involved. Perhaps, the most
satisfactory solution will be some mixture of market transfers
to rights and administrative allocations [8].

In any case, an appraisal of the historical effectiveness of
the market system to cope with past allocation problems would
be of marked value in gathering information about the necessary modifications to be introduced in the future.

The Problem of Pricing

A vital problem in the transfer of water between uses and
users is the formulation of a system or method of pricing that
adequately reflects the costs of supplying the water and the
value of alternative uses that are foregone. In any account of
the existing competition for water, consideration should be
accorded to making much greater use of prices and charges
in the allocation of water among competing demands. However,
as the previous discussion has shown, the nature of water
management and water values precludes complete or exclusive
reliance on market forces. This, of course, does not mean that
traditional policies and concepts should be allowed to inhibit
unduly the use of fees and charges in cases where market forces
can operate effectively in the optimization of economic values.
However, economists and policy-makers agree that the price
mechanism has serious limitations as a value indicator.

A significant problem in the transfer of water when both
public and private agencies are involved relates to the determination of the value of public goods. If water is priced, the
marginal value of the last unit of water to consumers is being
measured if the pricing is competitive. On the other hand, if
water is freely distributed, the factor cost of water production

measures the value of resources employed in water development in their highest alternative uses. The results obtained in each case will be different.

In the first instance, it is reasonable to assume that as a result of its market pricing, fewer resources would be devoted to the production of water in case of reduced demand and more to the generation of other items of output than in the second case. The composition of output in the two situations, therefore, differs. Consequently, judgments concerning appropriate weights have to be made to achieve an index number comparison.

Three factors stand out as dominant variables in public water pricing policies. These are: location of delivery (in relation to the head of a surface distribution system), the type of use to which water is put and time. Price may be systematically related to any or all of these variables or may be functionally unrelated.

The price aspect of water transfer potentially performs two economic functions, the efficiency of which may be evaluated. The first is allocating the involved resource; the second relates to investments in water "production," or more simply, the water-producing projects. Criteria for economic efficiency of the latter function include least-cost production and correct supply response. Marginal cost pricing may satisfy most of these criteria.

If there are "externalities," marginal cost pricing, however, will not suffice. One argument maintains that under such circumstances, marginal cost pricing coupled with a subsidization program financed by tax receipts is the most desirable way out. This position assumes that higher-cost firms will tend to be eliminated through market competition. In the case of water transfer, there is little opportunity for competition among producers. Rather, competition exists between agencies with regard to their scale of operation, with resulting internal pressures and, in the extreme, free water. Even with subsidization, the quantity demanded will not proceed to the point of zero marginal value productivity of water so long as any user price is charged [7].

Kelso points out that when water is developed by the government and sold to individuals, the price is usually determined by a mixture of ability to pay and the repayment necessary to cover the cost that has been allocated to this particular water use [6]. For example, the price of irrigation water to farmers on a Bureau of Reclamation project has little resemblance to the price that would exist in a free market situation. Thus, water prices need not necessarily reflect the differing productivities of water in different uses.

WATER TRANSFER: EFFICIENCY VS EQUITY

Various efforts have been made from time to time to formulate a water resources policy designed to maximize the returns from the allocation of water among competing uses. Economists have developed a body of theory to apply to situations in which the competitive market is not able to accomplish an efficient result. This body of theory, referred to as welfare economics, is directly applicable to water resources because of several characteristics of water development. Three of the principal characteristics are:

1. Many resource commodities can be produced and/or distributed at minimum cost only through natural monopolies because the conditions of production involve major economies of scale. Thus, the unregulated market does not function or functions only imperfectly in these instances.

2. Many products of water resources or water resource–connected services are not subject to division into units for sale and purchase. Flood control, for example, usually cannot be limited to a single piece of property, and a scenic area may be viewed by many.

3. Many uses of water resources have unusually significant spillover or external effects. Storage

of water at one location on a river influences power output at another location downstream. Use of a stream for waste disposal may be distinctly advantageous to a city or plant, but such use may impose costs or damages upon others downstream [5].

The theory of economic welfare can be systematically applied to spell out the conditions essential to achieve efficiency of activities possessing these characteristics.

A transfer process designed to allocate a limited or scarce resource to the highest competing or the most productive use may be regarded as efficient. To assess the efficiency of the transfer process, the duration of the rate of growth also has to be taken into account. For instance, a very rapid short-run growth may be socially less desirable than a somewhat lower rate of growth over a longer period.

A more difficult problem relates to the impact of water transfer on the question of equity. The effect of specific types of water transfer on income distribution, either directly or indirectly, through changes in real output is one of the principal aspects to be considered. Equitable economic growth, for the purposes of this analysis, is regarded as representing a positive rate of change in the real output of an economy with a smaller aggregate variation from the mean on a per capita basis. A per capita definition of equitable growth may not, however, be adequate. For example, regional income differences may be increased, although on a per capita basis it may appear that equity criteria are fulfilled. In studying the growth process from a long-term perspective, therefore, economic implications of such regional inequities which appear over time through the political processes are considerable, and they must be taken into account.

REFERENCES

1.   Wollman, N. *The Value of Water in Alternative Uses* (Albuquerque, NM: University of New Mexico Press, 1962).

2. Renshaw, E. F. "Value of Acre Foot of Water," *J. Am. Water Works Assoc.* 50(3):304 (1958).

3. Criddle, W. D. "Problems of Transferring Currently Developed Water Among Uses and Users," in *Water Transfer Problems,* Report No. 10, Conference Proceedings of the Committee on the Economics of Water Resource Development (Portland, OR: WAERC, 1961), pp. 21-24.

4. Hartman, L. M., and D. A. Seastone. "Welfare Goals and Organization of Decision Making for the Allocation of Water Resources," *Land Econ.* 41(1):21.

5. Fox, I. K. "New Horizons in Water Resources Administration," *Public Admin. Rev.* 25(1) (1965).

6. Kelso, M. M. "The Economics of Water Transfer: An Appraisal of Institutions," Regional Project Outline Unpublished (1964).

7. Brewer, M. "Water Transfer and Economic Growth," in *Water Transfer Problems,* Report No. 10, Conference Proceedings of the Committee on the Economics of Water Resource Development (Portland, OR: WAERC, 1961), p. 82.

8. Kneese, A. V. "Economic and Related Problems in Contemporary Water Resources Management," *Nat. Res. J.* 5(2):5(1965).

CHAPTER 2

THE DOCTRINE OF PRIOR APPROPRIATION AND ITS IMPACT ON WATER DEVELOPMENT: A CRITICAL SURVEY

INTRODUCTION

The strategic role of water in the development of the semi-arid and arid regions is nowhere more manifest than in the legal doctrines governing its development and use. This chapter attempts to study critically the legal framework encompassing water-resource development in the western United States. First, the doctrine of prior appropriation, the basic water law employed by the 17 states west of the Mississippi, is described in historical perspective. This is followed by a discussion of the principal features of the prior appropriation doctrine and a brief analysis of some of their implications for the economy and the society. This serves as an appropriate background to the next section, which attempts to illustrate the general theory discussed above, with specific examples from a number of western states. The analysis deals with surface- and ground-water laws separately, and presents supportive evidence to the conclusion that the doctrine of prior appropriation has through the years evolved into a fairly dynamic body of laws whose operational efficiency has increased considerably in the context of the rapidly expanding water needs of the western United States.

BACKGROUND

The doctrine of prior appropriation is generally regarded as governing the control and use of water in the 17 states west of the Mississippi (Arizona, California, Colorado, Idaho, Kansas, Montana, Nebraska, Nevada, New Mexico, North Dakota, Oklahoma, Oregon, South Dakota, Texas, Utah, Washington and Wyoming). However, only eight intermountain states—Arizona, Colorado, Idaho, Montana, Nevada, New Mexico, Utah and Wyoming—actually employ prior appropriation to the exclusion of the riparian doctrine. Oregon is also listed with these states because it has given up the riparian doctrine except for its application in a few early cases in which riparian rights were established for beneficial uses. The remaining eight western states employ a blend which recognizes some features of both systems. In other words, the appropriation principle is used in combination with the riparian doctrine.

Almost all of the western states are either arid or semiarid. In other words, the overall water supply in these states is always insufficient to grow crops on all the land available. There are, however, scattered areas of perennial water surplus within the region, chiefly along the north Pacific Coast and high in the mountain ranges. Except for these "purple patches," most of the West is basically water-short. Viewed in this perspective, the critical importance of water for agriculture in the West becomes self-evident.

The quantity of water available is far short of the quantity that would be required for farming all agricultural lands. The need for irrigation varies widely; and the primary consideration in a given area is the deficiency of precipitation during the growing season compared to the quantity of water required for crop growth. In some portions of the West, then, irrigation is seldom required; in others, it contributes to a wider range of crop production and to greater production than would be possible with complete dependence on precipitation; and in still others, it is necessary for practically every form of dependable agricultural development [1].

Much of the problem, therefore, stems from the simple fact that there is more land than water in the West [2]. Webb brings the whole situation into bold relief with the following observation:

> An examination of the rainfall map of the United States reveals clearly that the Great Plains environment has a far lower water supply than is found in the region east of the 98th meridian. From the time that men first crossed the line as explorers down to the present, there has been in this region a constant and persistent search for water [3].

Thus, it was pointed out as far back as 1931 that if every drop of water which falls on the mountains of the West could be made available, there would not be enough to supply half of the land suited for irrigation [3]. The situation has not changed significantly since then.

As people began to settle in the arid lands of the western states, it became increasingly clear that the riparian doctrine which prevails in most of the eastern United States was basically unsuited to the conditions in the West. Thus began the search for a new water law which would recognize the role of water in the development of these areas.

This system originated in the West in the mid-nineteenth century, where water was scarce and laws were rudimentary or often times nonexistent. It grew from the practice of the early settlers of taking water where they found it and using it where they needed it. In the course of time, and by common agreement, a crude system of notice was adopted to indicate the amount taken by and the nature of the use of each appropriator [4].

DOCTRINE OF PRIOR APPROPRIATION: THEORY

The principal features of the appropriation doctrine are:

1. It gives an exclusive right to the first appropriator; and, in accordance with the doctrine of priority, the

rights of later appropriations are conditional on the prior rights of those who have preceded.

2. It makes all rights conditional on beneficial use—as the doctrine of priority was adopted for the protection of the first settlers in time of scarcity, so the doctrine of beneficial use became a protection to later appropriators against wasteful use by those with earlier rights.

3. It permits water to be used on nonriparian lands as well as on riparian lands.

4. It permits diversion regardless of the diminution of the stream.

5. Continuation of the right depends upon beneficial use. The right may be lost by nonuse [5].

The basic principle underlying the appropriation doctrine is summed up by the catch phrase "first in time, first in right." This suggests that the key feature of the appropriation doctrine is its recognition of priorities in appropriative rights. Barlowe illustrates the operation of these priorities with the aid of a diagram depicting a stream upon which several claims for water have been filed (Figure 1).

It is assumed in Figure 1 that the first and sixth claims involve riparian users who take water to irrigate relatively small acreages, that the second and fifth priorities are held by irrigation projects along the stream, that the fourth priority involves a large irrigation project located several miles away from the stream, and that the third priority is held by a downstream hydroelectric plant which claims a definite minimum flow of the stream at all times.

Regardless of their location along the stream, each of these claimants enjoys water rights only in accordance with the priority of his (or its) claim. The first and second claimants may take water up to the full amount of their claims at any time. After them, the power company can insist upon a minimum natural flow of the stream, which may take all of the flow during drought periods. Because the priorities of the first three claimants may entitle them to the full flow of the stream during the

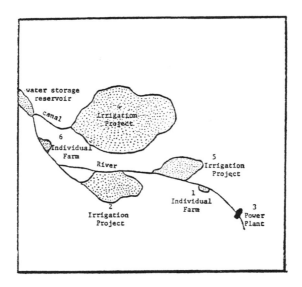

Figure 1. Example showing priorities in appropriative rights under the appropriation doctrine (source: Barlowe, R. *Land Resource Economics* (Englewood Cliffs, NJ:Prentice-Hall, Inc., 1961), p. 358).

drier months of the year, the remaining claimants can find their rights cut off at the very time they feel the greatest need for irrigation water. They can remedy this situation by building an upstream storage reservoir which will hold seasonal floodwater for later use [6].

The appropriation doctrine has been designed from the start to deal with a short-supply situation. However, it has not succeeded fully in accomplishing this task in the various western states that face an almost perennial water shortage.

PRIOR APPROPRIATION IN THE WESTERN STATES: PRACTICE

The purpose of this section is to study the actual operation of the doctrine of prior appropriation in a number of western states and to point out the modifications that have been effect-ed by these states to enhance its operational efficiency.

A review of the actual implementation of the appropriation doctrine in the several Western states leads to the following conclusions:

1. Administrative procedure governing the acquisition, deter-mination and administration of rights, in contrast with its early stages, has become highly developed through the West. The pre-sent procedures are based largely upon those which originated in Colorado and Wyoming. The state's supervision and control are usually exercised through the state engineer or other corres-ponding official, and the courts. In some states a board or depart-ment of the state government exercises control.

2. The centralized system of public control over water rights has not been completely applied in all states and has been more successful in some places than in others. However, it is a workable system generally and its foundation is the state's vital interest in the orderly utilization of its resources.

3. Many of the states have specifically dedicated unappro-priated waters to the public. Dedication of waters to the public, for the purposes of laying the legal foundation for their appro-priation and use under state regulation, is made by constitu-tional provision in some states but by statute in most of the states in the West. Some of the provisions refer to all waters in the state, and some speak of certain classes only. Such dedication of water is subject to vested private rights, as well as to the rights of the federal government [1].

For the sake of analytical clarity the application of the appropriation doctrine with reference to surface water and groundwater is considered separately.

Surface Water Rights

The doctrine of prior appropriation, in one form or another, constitutes the basis of the water laws relating to the ownership, control and appropriation of surface waters in most western states. Whatever changes have been made are mostly alterations to suit the special conditions obtaining in the different states.

Thus, the basic purpose behind these modifications was to enhance the operational efficiency of the original doctrine.

Arizona provides a typical example of a western state which has repudiated the riparian doctrine in clear terms and has based its water laws on the doctrine of appropriative rights. The courts have specifically held, time and again, that the riparian doctrine has been repudiated. However, for nearly three decades no efforts were made by the Territorial Government to regulate the manner in which a valid appropriation should be made. The determination of the methods for a valid appropriation was left entirely to the courts. The State Water Code of 1919 wrote into the legal structure of the state the principles which had governed the decisions of courts for many decades [7].

The doctrine of appropriation governs the acquisition of water rights in Colorado to the exclusion of the riparian doctrine. This was settled as far back as 1882 in *Coffin v. Left Hand Ditch Company* when the court stated:

> We conclude, then, that the common law doctrine giving the riparian owner a right to the flow of water in its natural channel upon and over his lands, even though he makes no beneficial use thereof, is inapplicable to Colorado. Imperative necessity, unknown to the countries which gave it birth, compels the recognition of another doctrine in conflict therewith [8].

In 1922 the U.S. Supreme Court, concerning Colorado and Wyoming, stated: "The common law rule respecting riparian rights in flowing water never obtained in either state." On the basis of these and a number of other court decisions, Hutchins concludes that Colorado had at no time recognized the riparian doctrine [1].

California has long recognized both the riparian doctrine and the doctrine of appropriation. The California Civil Code provides that all waters within the state are the property of the people of the state, and that running water flowing in a river or stream or down a canyon or ravine is subject to appropriation [9]. This resulted in a unique situation because it attempted to combine two systems of water rights that are inherently in conflict. The inevitable result was extensive litigation. As one writer points out:

> California's recognition of riparian rights in surface streams created an unavoidable conflict with use under appropriation rights for which a basis of compromise was not found until there has been 40 years of litigation [10].

However, the conflicts between the water systems finally began to be resolved and eventually the state has been able to evolve a highly workable system of water rights.

Out of the experience of the first hundred years of statehood, California had developed a workable water rights system under which those using water could determine the security of their title to their use and those planning projects to use unappropriated water could predict, with reasonable certainty, the water which might be available for use [10].

In 1913 the California Legislature enacted a general Water Commission Act covering all uses of water. This act (which became effective in December 1914) and the subsequent amendments form the basic statute governing appropriation rights in surface streams. The Water Commission Act was codified in 1943 as a part of the water code.

Groundwater Rights

Groundwater, technically, refers to all available water supplies under the surface of the earth: "all water in the ground that is free to move by gravity and to enter wells, capable of being extracted from the ground and susceptible to practicable legal control" [1]. Groundwater occurs through the precipitation and absorption of surface waters, including those flowing in streams, and it is continually in motion from higher to lower areas because of geological conditions and hydrostatic forces.

From a legal standpoint, groundwater is usually divided into two categories: (1) water flowing in defined subterranean streams, and (2) percolating, i.e., water flowing in channels reasonably ascertainable.

Groundwater hydrologists have criticized the above classification of groundwater into two distinct categories as having no scientific basis or satisfactory applicability [11]. For example, Thompson of the U.S. Geological Survey points out that "much of the classification of groundwater adopted in many court decisions and by writers of legal textbooks is not consistent with scientific principles of ground water hydrology" [1]. Consequently, this distinction has been removed from the water rights statutes of a number of western states, e.g., Idaho, Kansas, Nevada, Oregon, Utah, Wyoming, and North and South Dakota. However, several states, including both California and Texas, "with their great developments of groundwater for various purposes and their millions of acres of irrigated land" still retain this historical distinction. Even though the judicial distinction between groundwater streams and percolating waters lacks a scientific basis, still it has been employed in almost all legal discussions of groundwater.

The rights of individuals in groundwater spring from two contrasting doctrines of law: (1) The common law or English doctrine which emphasizes that the water is the absolute property of the owner of the overlying land in perpetuity; and (2) The doctrine of prior appropriation, whose fundamental principle is that the "first in time is the first in right" [12].

Water rights play a decisive role as far as the optimum use of the ground water resources is concerned. Hutchins, while discussing the relations of the individual rights to the public interest, points out that protection of private rights of property is a matter of public concern, because constitutional rights are invoked in securing the individual's rights.

Substantial private rights will be and should be protected. This is in the public interest. On the other hand, the perpetuation of unsubstantial unused and ill-used rights in an overdrawn groundwater reservoir is not in the public interest. Recent high court decisions, few though they are, indicate a growing awareness of this [13].

In many western states the use of underground streams is governed by the same water rights doctrine that is applied to surface waters. For instance, if a definite underground stream is found in a riparian doctrine state, its waters are normally subject to the riparian rights recognized in that state. Likewise, if the underground stream is located in an appropriation or modified riparian doctrine state, its waters in most cases are available for appropriation [6].

With such exceptions and exemptions, statutes invoking the doctrine of prior appropriation have been applied to all groundwaters in Colorado, Idaho, Kansas, Nevada, New Mexico, Oklahoma, Oregon, South Dakota, Utah, Washington and Wyoming. Arizona applies the doctrine in declared "critical areas" for use of water on newly developed land. In California, the doctrine applies to groundwater that may be surplus to the needs of overlying landowners and that are proposed to be exported beyond the basin of origin [12].

Hutchins points out in his discussion of groundwater legislation that the English rule was replaced in some states by the American rule of reasonable use.

This rule recognizes the landowner's right to capture and use the water that exists in his land, but limits him to such quantity of water as is necessary for some useful purpose in connection with the land from which the water is extracted. The chief limitations are that waste of the water or export of the water for distant use are not reasonable if the result deprives other overlying landowners of the opportunity to make reasonable use of the common supply on their own land [13].

How precisely does the doctrine of prior appropriation operate with respect to the control and use of groundwater? Figure 2 illustrates this succinctly [14].

New Mexico has a highly regarded groundwater code which asserts public ownership of the groundwaters of the state and provides for their apportionment in the public interest. New Mexico Appropriative Groundwater Statute was the first to be put into wide administrative operation, and it has established a general pattern for much of the subsequent legislation of that sort. The statute, first enacted in 1927, was ruled invalid

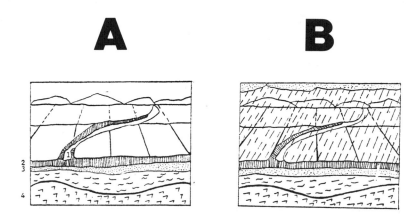

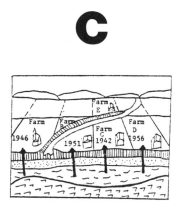

Figure 2. An example of prior appropriation. **(A)** A cross section of subsurface (1) stream or dry stream bed, (2) layer of topsoil, (3) previous material—sand, gravel, etc., (4) underground material—rock, shale. **(B)** Recharge by rainfall and seepage downward to subsurface area. **(C)** Appropriation of water. Farmers A, B, C and D have appropriated groundwater in the years 1946, 1951, 1942 and 1956, respectively. Farmer E decides to apply. If the state has a system for controlling appropriations of groundwater, the administrator will decide prior appropriation, and the application may be decided by a local administrator or by the courts through an adjudication. If groundwater levels are lowered to an excessive extent, the latest appropriators may be ordered, in reverse order of appropriation, to stop pumping until the situation is alleviated. The first in time is the first in right (source: *Oklahoma's Water Resources* (Oklahoma City, OK: Oklahoma Water Resources Board, 1960), p. 33).

because of technical defects, and was replaced by the current statute enacted in 1931 and amended by additions in 1953. Basic provisions of the statute are given below:

> 7-11-1. The water of underground streams, channels, artesian basins, reservoirs, or lakes, having reasonably ascertainable boundaries, and hereby declared to be public waters and to belong to the public and to be subject to appropriation for beneficial use. (Modified by 75-11-9 and 75-11-21, below.)
>
> 75-11-2. Beneficial use is the basis, the measure, and the limit of the right to the use of the (ground) waters.
>
> 75-11-9. All underground waters of the State of New Mexico are hereby declared to be public waters and to belong to the public of the State of New Mexico and to be subject to appropriation for beneficial use within the State of New Mexico. All existing rights to the beneficial use of such waters are hereby recognized.
>
> 7-11-20. No person shall withdraw water from any underground source in the State of New Mexico for use in any other state by drilling a well in New Mexico and transporting the water outside the state or by drilling a well outside the boundaries of the state and pumping water from under lands lying within the territorial boundaries of the State of New Mexico.
>
> 75-11-21. No permit and license to appropriate underground waters shall be required except in basins declared by the state engineer to have reasonably ascertainable boundaries.
>
> 75-11-22. The state engineer and the attorney general or the various district attorneys are authorized and directed to use any and all legal means necessary to enforce the provisions of (the act).

In 1950, the constitutionality of the New Mexico statute was challenged, but the court upheld its validity. The challengers argued that the waters at issue were their absolute property, since they were owners of the overlying land (invoking the principle of the common law doctrine). The court maintained, however, that the Desert Land Act of 1877 had set apart those waters for disposition by the state.

The appropriation doctrine, no doubt, is regarded as the sole basis for a right to surface or groundwater in New Mexico. It is interesting to note, however, that the state supreme court in 1958 decreed that the town of Las Vegas had a paramount right to all the water required for its continued growth, on the basis of a Mexican colonization (Pueblo) grant in 1835 [15].

In Texas the use of groundwater is regulated by the common law doctrine. The state authorizes groups of water users to form conservancy districts for "the conservation, preservation, protection and recharging and the prevention of waste of the underground water of an underground water reservoir or subdivision thereof" [16]. In the high plains area of Texas, districts have actually been formed and are operating under this act [17].

Groundwater plays a dominant role in the overall water supply of Arizona. For example, as much as 70% of the total water used for irrigation in the state in 1952 came from groundwater sources, causing a considerable lowering of the groundwater level. The first serious attempt to regulate the use of groundwater in Arizona found expression in the form of the Ground Water Code of 1948. This water code, however, suffered from serious defects, and in 1951 a committee was appointed to study the groundwater situation and to recommend methods of strengthening the water code. The recommendation of the Underground Water Commission was that there was great need for regulatory legislation to prevent further excessive discharges of groundwater. However, no serious effort seems to have been made in this direction. Mann has summed up very well the existing situation with respect to groundwater use in Arizona:

> Ground water laws have perhaps prevented the expansion of agriculture and further over-development of land dependent on ground water, but they have not redressed the serious imbalance of withdrawal and supply that existed before the laws were put on statute books [7].

The groundwater law in Nevada is based on "preferential use" [18]. This resembles closely the "highest and best use" of the modified doctrine of riparian rights. The incorporation of "preferential use" into the groundwater law of Nevada is, in part, an attempt to solve the problem of groundwater basin discharges. These discharges have resulted in marked reduction in the capacity of the reservoir, cracking of masonry and concrete floors, ruptures of pipe lines leading from walls, damage to pumping equipment, broken water lines and cracked curbs and streets.

Under this authorization (Nevada State Law NRS534·120, Art. 2), the drilling of irrigation wells has been prohibited in the highly developed part of Las Vegas, although municipal and domestic wells still may be drilled. The state also has recognized preferential use of water for domestic use in that a maximum of 1440 gal/day per household may be withdrawn for domestic use without regard to other water rights [19].

The basic rule that governs the rights to the use of groundwater in California is an outgrowth of the American rule of reasonable use known as the *California Correlative Doctrine,* or doctrine of correlative rights. This doctrine implies that:

> The rights of all landowners over a common basin, saturated strata or underground reservoir are co-equal or correlative, and that one landowner may not extract more than his share even for use on his own lands, where the rights of others are injured thereby; nor can he claim more than this share on the ground of peculiar benefit to him from its use.

Thus, rights of use under this doctrine are based on location of the land in relation to the water supply. In other words, owners of all lands that overlie a supply of percolating water have correlative or coequal rights to the use of the water, just as have the owners of riparian lands in the waters of the stream to which their lands are contiguous [20].

CONCLUSIONS

The appropriation doctrine has been gaining increasing importance in recent years, even in some of the eastern states. The reason for this stems from some of the distinct advantages of this system. Martin gives a lucid account of some of these advantages:

> Among these, the principle of full utilization of the water resources deserves to be ranked first. Second, the appropriation system permits the use of water where needed without tying use to riparian ownership. Third, it restricts the appropriator to beneficial use, both as to purpose and as to amount and makes possible the reappropriation of excess amounts not beneficially used. Fourth, the amount, purposes and place of use of appropriated water are definitely indicated, and this adds an element of certainty which is unknown under the riparian system. Fifth, management of water resources by the courts through individual case rulings gives way under appropriation to management by a full-time administrative agency staffed by experts [4].

The foregoing discussion suggests that the doctrine of prior appropriation has been successful to a large degree in adapting itself to meet the changing and challenging water requirements of the American West. The changes have occurred gradually, but steadfastly and, what is more, they have permeated the patterns of ownership and distribution of both surface and groundwaters. Admittedly, significant rigidities are built into the body of western water laws, and considerable scope exists for further improvement and modification. However, it is clear from the above analysis that the doctrine of prior appropriation has, over the years, undergone numerous changes and adaptations which indubitably point to the conclusion that it has not remained a moribund body of archaic regulations, but has often been characterized by a fair measure of vigor and dynamism.

REFERENCES

1. Hutchins, W. A. *Selected Problems in the Law of Water Rights in the West,* U.S. Department of Agriculture, Miscellaneous Publication 418, Washington, DC (1942), pp. 64-65.
2. Hodge, C., Ed., *Aridity and Man,* Publication No. 74 (Washington, DC: American Association for the Advancement of Science, 1963).
3. Webb, W. P. *The Great Plains* (New York: Grosset & Dunlap, 1931), p. 319.
4. Martin, R. C. *Water for New York* (Syracuse, NY: Syracuse University Press, 1960), p. 109.
5. Huffman, R. *Irrigation Development and Public Water Policy* (New York: The Ronald Press Company, 1953), p. 43.
6. Barlowe, R. *Land Resource Economics* (Englewood Cliffs, NJ: Prentice-Hall, Inc., 1961), p. 358.
7. Mann, D. E. *The Politics of Water in Arizona* (Tucson, AZ: University of Arizona Press, 1963), p. 38.
8. Six Colorado 443 (1882).
9. California Civil Code (Sec. 1410).
10. Harding, S. T. *Water in California* (Palo Alto, CA: N. P. Publication, 1960), p. 26.
11. Thompson, D. G. and A. G. Fiedler. "Some Problems Relating to Legal Control of Use of Groundwaters," *J. Am. Water Works Assoc.,* 30:1049-61.
12. Piper, A. M. "Interpretation and Current Status of Ground Water Rights," paper presented at the Water Rights Conference, Michigan State University, East Lansing, MI, March 1960, p. 68.
13. Hutchins, W. A. "Groundwater Legislation," *Rocky Mountain Law Rev.* 30(4):440 (1958).
14. Oklahoma Water Resources Board, *Oklahoma's Water Resources* (Oklahoma City: 1960), p. 33.
15. Harold E. Thomas, "Essentials for Optimum Use of Ground Water Resources," *Western Resources Conference 1959* (Boulder: Univ. of Colorado Press, 1960), p. 184.
16. Texas Laws. "Underground Water-Bill," Sec. 3c (1949).
17. Duggan, G. "Texas Groundwater Law," "Proceedings 1954," University of Texas Water Law Conference.
18. U.S. Geological Survey. "The Groundwater Situation in Nevada, 1970," U.S. Department of the Interior (1961), p. 6.
19. Malmberg, G. T. "Land Subsidence in Las Vergas Valley, Nevada," U.S. Geological Survey, U.S. Department of the Interior (1964), p. 6.
20. Hutchins, W. A. "California Groundwater: Legal Problems," *California Law Rev.* (December 1957), p. 689.

CHAPTER 3

MULTINATIONAL CORPORATIONS, NATION-STATES AND OCEAN RESOURCE MANAGEMENT: THE IMPACT OF A 200-MILE ECONOMIC ZONE

INTRODUCTION

Multinational corporations (MNC) are today one of the most significant and potent institutions in the context of international resource development and management. Recent investigations clearly point to a remarkable burgeoning of interest on the part of MNC in oceans and their rich and varied resources, especially offshore oil.

Concurrently, the role of the nation-state in ocean resource development is on the verge of gaining a dramatic upsurge. A development of special importance in this context is the pronounced and rapidly growing sentiment both in the United States and abroad in favor of extending the national jurisdiction over ocean resources to 200 nautical miles. More than 40 countries, among them the United States, Japan, Canada, New Zealand, Australia, Mexico, India and the Philippines have already enacted legislation creating either a 200-mile fishing and conservation zone or a full-fledged 200-mile economic zone. At the Sixth Session of the Third United Nations Law of the Sea Conference, held in New York in the summer of 1977, there was unanimous agreement about the rights of the coastal nations to declare a 200-mile economic zone, although the question of defining its precise nature is not fully settled. In any event, the 200-mile economic zone, in the words of Conference Chairman Ambassador H.S. Amerasinghe, is already "a fact of international law."

The purpose of this chapter is to examine the probable impact of a 200-mile exclusive economic zone on the pace and pattern of multinational as well as nation-state activity in the world oceans.

IMPACT OF EXTENDED JURISDICTION

The proposal to create a 200-mile economic zone over which the coastal states would have complete jurisdiction represents a major change in the prevailing system of ocean resource ownership and management. Under the present system, ocean resources in the waters beyond the 12-mile territorial jurisdiction of the coastal states are regarded as common property resources. As such, no particular state enjoys exclusive control or sole ownership over the resources, living as well as nonliving, beyond the 12-mile limit. (This is not to ignore the fact that many nations have claimed jurisdiction over the continental shelf during the postwar period [e.g., Truman Proclamation of 1945 and the Geneva Continental shelf] out to the 200-m isobath). Consequently, considerable activity on the part of MNC, especially U.S.-, Soviet- and Japanese-based MNC, has until recently been taking place in "international waters." Entry to these waters, in most instances, was open, and no international code of conduct governing the operations of MNC has been in existence. The absence of regulatory legal and institutional mechanisms and economic sanctions has led to several instances of bitter feuds among corporations, as well as among governments. This state of anarchy has also resulted in poor allocation of resources and considerable waste.

The creation of a 200-mile economic zone which would give exclusive jurisdiction to coastal states over ocean resources up to 200 miles from the shore is bound to alter the above situation. Specifically, it is hypothesized that the following changes would occur:

1. transfer of a significant portion of ocean resources, especially fisheries, currently deemed "common property" to the jurisdiction of the nation-state;
2. a diminution in the competition among MNC of different countries for the resources in the ocean space previously deemed international; and
3. progressive escalation of controls over subsidiaries of multinationals by the host countries, many of which come under the category of "less-developed" countries.

The collective and more enduring impact of these developments, it is argued in this chapter, will be the creation of a new regime of natural resource development and management in a global context. Such a regime or order or arrangement could lead to a significant increase in the harmonization of the relationship between the MNC and the nation-states. This chapter attempts to challenge the conventional wisdom that the relationship between the MNC and the nation-states is, as a rule, one of conflict and competition, and that they must be treated as separate entities working in isolation and at cross purposes.

MNC AND NATION-STATES: PARTNERS IN DEVELOPMENT

The extension of coastal state jurisdiction to 200 nautical miles would lead to a unique situation in terms of the ownership of ocean resources; that is, 15 coastal states would receive among them approximately 42% of the world's 200-mile economic zone area [1] (Table I). What is even more intriguing is the fact that at least half of these countries are less-developed countries which would be dependent on MNC for the development and efficient management of their newly acquired ocean wealth.

Viewed against this backdrop, the emerging pattern of relationship between the nation-states and MNC is likely to be one of constructive partnership in development. Such cooperation is in the best interest of both parties, and is crucial to the optimum use of a large body of ocean resources in which both have a large stake. The reasons for this conclusion follow.

Table I. States with the Largest Economic Zones[a]

State	Economic Zone (Area) $(10^3$ nautical mi$^2)$
United States	2222
Australia	2043
Indonesia	1577
New Zealand	1409
Canada	1370
Soviet Union	1309
Japan	1126
Brazil	924
Mexico	831
Chile	667
Norway	590
India	587
Philippines	551
Portugal	517
Malagasy	377

[a]Source: Alexander and Hodgson [1].

At least half of the countries which stand to gain as a result of the extension of jurisdiction simply do not have the key factors: capital, technology and managerial skill essential to tap these resources (Table II).Examples of such less-developed coastal states (LDCS) are Indonesia, Mexico, India, Philippines and Portugal. A recent survey clearly points to a critical shortage of marine scientists and technologists in these countries [2]. And the immediate or even short-term prospect of these coastal states being able to optimally use their newly acquired ocean bounty without major assistance from developed coastal states (DCS) (e.g., the United States or Japan) does not appear very promising.

Table II. States with the Largest Economic Zones: A Comparative Perspective

State	Economic Zone (Area) (10^3 nautical mi^2)	Per Capita Income 1974 ($)	Scientific Manpower (1971)
DCS			
United States	2,222	6,640	528,000
Canada	1,370	6,080	19,200
Norway	590	5,280	3,760
Australia	2,043	4,760	10,000
New Zealand	1,409	4,100	1,000
Japan	1,126	3,880	160,000
Soviet Union	1,309	2,300	806,300
LDCS			
Portugal	517	1,540	500
Mexico	831	1,000	1,750
Brazil	924	900	8,000
Chile	667	820	3,500
Philippines	551	310	6,900
Malagasy	377	170	200
Indonesia	1,577	150	1,000
India	587	130	27,000

However, such assistance can hardly be provided by the governments or the public sectors of most DCS, because a considerable part of their marine technological expertise is in the domain of the private sector. Research in and development of ocean technology as it relates to offshore oil, deep-sea mining (e.g., manganese nodules) and fisheries have almost exclusively been undertaken by the private corporations, several of them MNC, using their own resources. This is particularly true of offshore oil production. The scope and dimensions of MNC involvement in oil production, including offshore oil production, are delineated in Table III. Consider also the fact that the risk associated with a number of marine resource exploitation ventures is very high, and consequently governmental assistance by way of capital is hard to come by in such cases. This situa-

Table III. MNC of Market Economies Engaged in Oil Production
with Sales of Over $1 Billion, 1971[a]

Company	Nationality	Total Sales ($ million)	Subsidiary Countries
Standard Oil (NJ)	U.S.	18,701	25
Royal Dutch/Shell Group	Neth/U.K.	12,734	43
Mobil Oil	U.S.	8,243	62
Texaco	U.S.	7,529	30
Gulf Oil	U.S.	5,940	61
British Petroleum	U.K.	5,191	52
Standard Oil of California	U.S.	5,143	26
Standard Oil (IN)	U.S.	4,054	24
Shell Oil (Sub. of Royal Dutch Shell)	U.S.	3,892	NA[b]
Atlantic Richfield	U.S.	3,135	12
Continental Oil	U.S.	3,051	27
Occidental Petroleum	U.S.	2,400	21
Cie Francaise des Petroles	France	2,395	28
Phillips Petroleum	U.S.	2,363	37
ENI	Italy	2,172	39
Union Oil of California	U.S.	1,981	NA
Sun Oil	U.S.	1,939	21
Ashland Oil	U.S.	1,614	17
Standard Oil (OH)	U.S.	1,394	NA
Petrofina	Belgium	1,350	21
Getty Oil	U.S.	1,343	19
Pemes (Petroleos Mexicanos)	Mexico	1,214	NA
Marathon Oil	U.S.	1,182	NA

[a]Source: Fatemi, N.S. et al. *Multinational Corporations: Problems and Prospects*
(New York: A. S. Barnes and Company, 1976).
[b]Not available.

tion further strengthens the role of MNC in the context of
helping to develop the vast ocean wealth of many of the LDCS.

The LDCS, however, do enjoy a good measure of power that
is derived from a combination of circumstances. First, under the
new legal regime, they would gain control of large amounts of
ocean resources, and as such MNC would require the express
permission of these countries to undertake any resource exploitation within their economic zones. Secondly, rapidly
rising demand for oil and metals like cobalt, copper and nickel

on the part of the DCS would further contribute to the bargaining power of the LDCS. In a global situation of progressive resource scarcities, MNC in developed coastal nations would find it ill-advised to engage in delaying tactics to get better terms from the LDCS, because time is a critical constraint. Finally, the fact that there has always been competition among the corporations of the different DCS to gain control of the precious marine resources of the LDCS should be taken into account. This is a situation that the latter can put to good use for eliciting favorable terms.

The arguments stemming from economic nationalism which have probably some validity in a variety of resource use and management contexts appear to have very little validity in the case of ocean resources. This is because MNC are not depriving entrepreneurs of LDCS of profitable investment opportunities in their home countries; if anything, MNC activity leads to the generation of new investment and employment opportunities, increased export earnings and improved balance-of-payments for these countries.

From the perspective of resource use optimization and externalities, LDCS stand to gain from enlisting the support of MNC. Multinational corporations in DCS, in turn, derive a number of benefits, including a high marginal efficiency of capital and ready access to much-needed resources, from investment in the ocean resource development programs of the LDCS.

What emerges from this discussion is thus a unique situation of strong interdependence, where the strengths of one party are the weaknesses of the other and vice versa. The opportunities for any serious exploitation of one party by the other are few, if any, and the inexorable logic of the situation dictates a relationship that would be most productive in a cooperative context. Any attempt at unilateral action detrimental to the interests of one party could turn out to be counterproductive and even disastrous. Thus, there are built-in safeguards and checks-and-balances inherent in the situation.

ALTERNATIVE FUTURES OF WORLD ORDER:
A THIRD DIMENSION

Discussions of alternative futures of world order and natural resource management have so far been largely "conducted in terms of two plausible models of world order: the nation state system and a world of corporate giants" [3]. Implicit in this approach is the notion that the two systems are competitive, mutually exclusive, at cross purposes to one another and, therefore, the relationship between the two is considered as an adversary relationship.

This is exemplified by the comments that have been made about the two systems by the protagonists of each. There are those who argue that the MNC pose a serious threat to the nation-state system, "the most accepted principle of world ordering today," [3] leading to a predicament where nation-states find themselves stripped of their sovereignty, their "sovereignty at bay" [4]. There are those who recognize the rapidly growing supremacy of the multinationals and express the view that in the final analysis, the negative impact of MNC far outweighs their positive impact. According to Galbraith, the multinational corporation "internationalizes the tendency to inequality" [5].

In sharp contrast are the views expressed by Ball, that the "nation-state is a very old-fashioned idea" [6], and even more bluntly by Kindleberger that "the nation-state is just about through as an economic unit" [7]. Tannenbaum goes a step further when he argues that the nation-state is becoming "functionless" [8], and that the MNC are forming the base for an alternative world order.

In all these comments, the notion of an adversary relationship, of conflict, competition and disharmony between the two systems, nation-states and MNC, runs like a red thread in a tapestry. An attempt is made here to point out that this need not be the case. An alternative scenario based on the emerging new regime of ocean resource use points to a situation in which the nation states and MNC are more likely to work in harmony, accord and constructive partnership. It is shown that the two entities would maximize their welfare and contribute to each other's development efforts in a positive, beneficial fashion by working as partners, not as rivals, in a total effort.

CONCLUSIONS

The emerging world order of tomorrow would more likely consist of a synergistic partnership of powerful nation-states and powerful multinational corporations, rather than an over-whelming dominance and subjugation of one by the other. The evolving reality of a world ocean regime, thus, is adding a new dimension to the traditional approach to alternative futures of world order.

REFERENCES

1. Alexander, L. M., and R. D. Hodgson. "The Impact of the 200-Mile Economic Zone on the Law of the Sea," *San Diego Law Rev.* 12(3): 574–575 (1975).
2. Qasim, S. Z. "Development of Marine Science Capabilities in Different Regions of the World," *Report of the Marine Science Workshop*, Bologna, Italy (1973).
3. Modelski, G. "Multinational Business: A Global Perspective," in *Multinational Corporations and World Order,* G. Modelski, Ed. (Beverly Hills, CA: Sage Publications, 1972).
4. Vernon, R. *Sovereignty at Bay* (New York: Basic Books, 1971).
5. Galbraith, J. K. *Economics and the Public Purpose* (Boston, MA: Houghton Mifflin, 1973).
6. Ball, G. "The Promise of the Multinational Corporation," *Fortune* 75:80 (1971).
7. Kindleberger, C. *American Business Abroad* (New Haven: CT: Yale University Press, 1969).
8. Brown, C., Ed. *World Business: Promise and Problems* (New York: MacMillan Publishing Co., Inc., 1970).

CHAPTER 4

ESTIMATING ENERGY REQUIREMENTS FOR AGRICULTURE: SOME METHODOLOGICAL ISSUES*

INTRODUCTION

Until recently, the need for accurate energy use data in agriculture had received only scant attention from agricultural scientists. However, in the wake of the recent energy shortages in the United States, there has been a growing recognition of the critical importance of such information for agricultural planning and development. There is currently a severe dearth of reliable information on the direct as well as indirect energy requirements for the different sectors of the agricultural economy. This has made meaningful projections of future energy needs for the different crops and livestock an exceedingly difficult task. In the absence of such estimations, formulation of a viable energy policy for the U.S. agricultural sector would be next to impossible. The recognition of the need for reliable energy use data in agriculture has led to some noteworthy contributions in the last few years [1-8].

The first collective effort to identify major research needs in this area and to develop useful new information was initiated in July 1974 in the form of a regional research project entitled, "Energy in Western Agriculture: Requirements, Adjustments and Alternatives." The central objectives of this project are:

*Co-authored with Neil Patrick.

49

1. to estimate current patterns and amounts of energy inputs used in Western agriculture;
2. to examine and analyze adjustments which might result from changes in forms and supplies of energy resources and consequent impacts on Western agriculture; and
3. to assess contributions of and prospects for alternative technologies and policies for dealing with changes in energy availability.

ENERGY REQUIREMENTS ESTIMATION

This chapter is concerned primarily with the first of the objectives mentioned above. Pilot studies of energy requirements for wheat in California, beef in New Mexico and sugarcane in Hawaii have been completed, and similar studies for other agricultural products are currently underway in a number of Western states. The experience from these studies as well as the insights gained from other published research clearly suggest the need for greater coordination and uniformity in the techniques of collecting, analyzing and reporting energy use data in agriculture.

The estimation of energy requirements for agriculture is beset with problems of definition and scope. Perhaps the paramount problem involves the definition of agriculture. The term agriculture is used in this discussion in a broad sense to represent all products resulting from the photosynthetic process consisting of the traditional crop and livestock food products, fiber, forest products and fisheries.

Another significant problem relates to the delineation of the scope of agriculture. Where do we start accounting for the energy required to manufacture agricultural inputs? Should the energy needed to extract and refine iron ore that eventually goes into farm machinery be allocated to agriculture? At what stage of consumption should we cease allocating energy used to agriculture? Do we account for the energy required to heat water and wash dishes or to dispose of garbage?

ENERGY FLOW MODEL FOR AGRICULTURE

In an attempt to find answers to such questions, an energy flow model for agriculture (Figure 1) has been developed.

On the left side, the energy flow model begins with the manufacture of agricultural inputs. Energy requirements should not be charged to agriculture until the point in the manufacturing process when the product is clearly destined to be used in agriculture. For instance, the energy consumed in steel manufacturing should not be allocated to agriculture before the point it is fabricated into a tractor or agricultural implement. Before this point, the steel could be used for any of a number of uses or products.

The flow model ends on the right side of Figure 1 with the energy required for final preparation of food in the home or total energy consumed by away-from-home dining establishments. According to this definition, all energy used for food preparation and storage, as well as that required for heating, cooling and lighting in dining establishments away from home will be included in the estimation of energy requirements. However, energy involved in food consumption at home should include only that used for storage and preparation.

Stages

The energy flow model in Figure 1 depicts a general model of agriculture. Most agricultural products can be traced through the entire model. Beef provides a good example of such a product. The manufacture of inputs that go into the production system consisting of such items as pesticides, drugs, feed preparation, delivery equipment and structures is included in Stage 1. The distribution of these inputs through the wholesale and retail markets to the farmers and ranchers raising beef is covered by Stage 2. Stage 3 encompasses the farm and ranch production of beef cattle. The initial marketing activity when the cattle leave the farm or ranch is represented by Stage 4. Beef slaughter, meat processing, aging, cutting and packaging are depicted

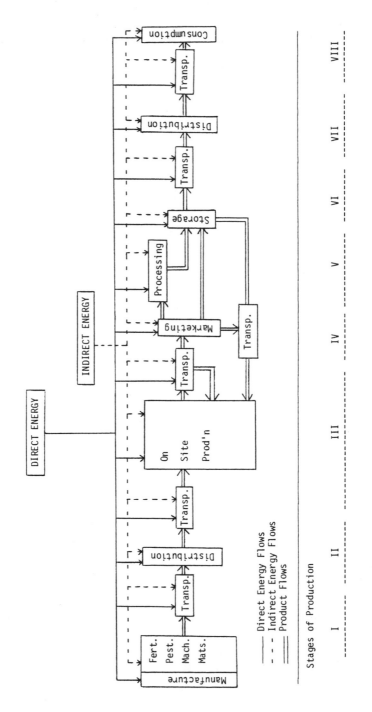

Figure 1. Energy flow model for agriculture (adapted from: "The U.S. Food and Fiber Sector, Energy Use and Outlook" [6].)

by Stage 5. The storage phase, Stage 6, involves the time interval between processing of beef and its transfer to the wholesale and retail outlets represented by Stage 7. The final stage (Stage 8) in the flow model includes at-home and away-from-home beef consumption.

Some agricultural products do not follow through the entire model. For instance, most feed grains are recycled through livestock either within Stage 3 or returned to it after passing through one or more subsequent stages. Forages follow much the same pattern.

Note that between each stage of the model a transportation activity is indicated. Individual situations would determine whether the transportation activity is included in the initial or subsequent stages of the flow model. Transportation could also figure as a separate activity as in the case of independent transportation firms not linked to any specific stage.

Labor and water constitute unique inputs into the model. Labor is required in every stage. The energy cost of labor is associated with its transportation, to and from work. The energy costs of water distribution include the manufacture of machinery needed for pumping, the actual fuel used in the pumping process and the energy needed for the building of dams, canals and pipelines.

ECONOMIC ENERGY

Energy required in agriculture comes from many sources such as fossil fuels, nuclear, hydropower, geothermal, solar and wind. Our primary concern in the study of energy in agriculture should be directed toward those forms of energy that command a price. We call it "economic energy." Solar energy captured by plants through photosynthesis is considered a free good. Although wind power itself is free, some energy cost is involved in its capture. Hydropower presents somewhat the same situation as wind except for the fact that its energy cost of capture is much greater.

Economic energy as required by agriculture consists of two distinct categories: direct and indirect energy. Direct energy includes that energy consumed directly in the production process, for example, electricity, diesel fuel, liquefied petroleum gas (LPG), gasoline and coal. Indirect energy includes that energy consumed in the production of agricultural inputs. This category can be further divided into two subcategories: ancillary and embodied energy. Ancillary energy is that energy required to produce inputs consumed in a single activity or a production period, for example, fertilizers, chemicals and packaging materials. Embodied energy is that energy required to manufacture durable inputs such as tractors, machinery, buildings and refrigeration equipment.

DIMENSIONS OF ENERGY STUDIES

Viewed in light of the definition of agriculture used in this discussion, the question of determining the various dimensions of energy studies in agriculture would pose some difficult and intriguing problems. These problems have the following six dimensions: (1) product determination; (2) stages of production; (3) energy source; (4) levels of technology; (5) geographic areas; and (6) time. We will discuss each of these in some detail.

Product Determination

What constitutes a product, at which point in the production process can it be defined, and what units of measure to be employed are the principal problems with respect to product determination. The central issue is one of identifying a point in the production process which sets a base for the estimation of the total energy requirements.

Wheat can be used as an example. The point of identification could be any one of the following: grain, flour or bread (Figure 2). Each of these methods of product identification represents a different approach to the determination of energy require-

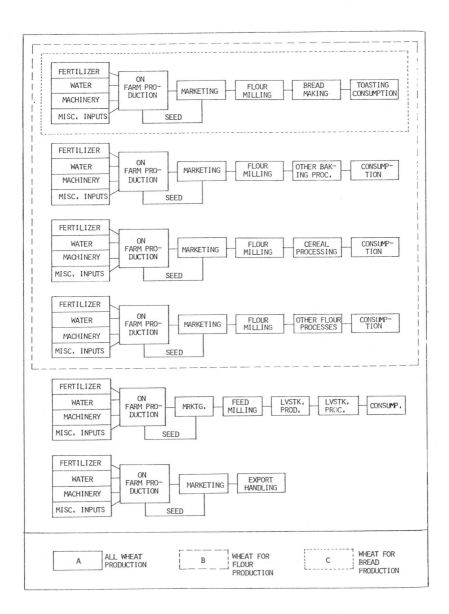

Figure 2. Alternative flow models of wheat production systems.

ments. The first approach would perhaps lead to three separate products such as hard winter wheat, soft spring wheat and durum wheat. The second approach would perhaps involve a half dozen or more products depending on the type of flour, coarseness of grind and degree of refining. This method would exclude grain exports as well as domestic uses for wheat other than flour. The problems are even more complex in the case of the third approach based on bread as the product identification point. There are perhaps a dozen or more types of bread produced from wheat flour. Further, this would eliminate all the nonbread uses of wheat from consideration, which are quite significant.

The above discussion points to the critical need for establishing a common reference point for each agricultural product. This would facilitate the process of focusing the energy requirements from all stages of production to a central unifying point. For example, this would enable the estimation of the total energy consumed from the U.S. energy budget by a given quantity of agricultural product as defined at this reference point. Perhaps the point of greatest product homogeneity should be used as the reference point of product determination. It would appear that for most agricultural products, this reference point would be when the product leaves Stage 3 (Figure 1), earlier defined as onsite production.

Stages of Production

A good deal of the information on energy requirements of agriculture completed in the past is of an aggregate nature and does not provide specific information for the various stages of production and the activities within these stages. Such information is vital to the formulation of realistic energy policies and planning. It is in this context that the significance of the stages approach presented in the energy flow model for agriculture becomes evident. By separating the production system into stages and defining them to have uniform scope, it would be possible to generate comparable and comprehensive information regarding energy requirements.

Each stage consists of a series of activities for which energy requirement data could be developed. For instance, the onsite production stage for sugarcane consists of a number of activities such as ground preparation, planting, cultural practices and harvesting. Even those could be further subdivided into more definitive operations. To illustrate, ground preparation consists of plowing, discing, etc. The logical conclusion is that energy requirements should be determined and reported at least to the extent of disaggregation represented by the stages.

Energy Source

Energy used in agriculture comes from a number of sources, each of which is unique in its characteristics with respect to its formation, transportation and use. Our primary concern here is with "economic energy," since this represents the forms which deplete the world's limited supply of nonrenewable energy.

All forms of economic energy consumed in the agricultural production process are derived from primary energy sources. For instance, gasoline, LPG, diesel and fuel oil are manufactured from crude oil by refining. This refining process involves the use of energy. Energy is also required for the distribution of these fuels to their ultimate consumption points. One unit of energy consumed in agricultural production, thus, represents more than one unit of primary energy, as high as 3.87 for electricity (Table I).

Table I. Inverse Energy Efficiency of Energy Production [9]

Energy Type	Btu Primary Energy/ Btu Delivered Energy
Coal	1.024
Refined Petroleum	1.208
Electricity	3.870
Natural Gas	1.169

It should be clear from this discussion that the actual drain on the nonrenewable energy supplies is considerably greater than the total energy at the farm and firm levels within agriculture. The degree of efficiency of primary energy use is thus determined by the mix of secondary energy sources used in the production process.

In reporting energy use, it is necessary to classify energy consumption into the two categories of direct and indirect energy discussed in an earlier section. The value of the information reported could be further enhanced by separating indirect energy into ancillary energy and embodied energy. An example of such distinction is provided by the New Mexico beef study shown in Figure 3.

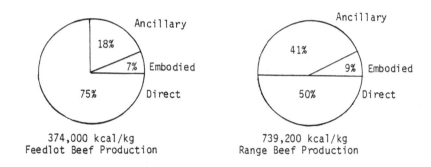

374,000 kcal/kg
Feedlot Beef Production

739,200 kcal/kg
Range Beef Production

Figure 3. Energy requirements for beef produced under range and feedlot conditions in New Mexico.

Currently, energy consumption is being reported using a bewildering array of units of measurement. Units of measurement range from joules to barrels of crude oil equivalent. For meaningful comparisons of energy consumption, it is essential to have a single, uniform unit of measurement. The use of kilocalories (kcal) is recommended.

Technology Types

There is close interrelationship between the amount of energy consumed in agricultural production and the type of technology employed. Thus, the actual energy consumed at each stage of the agricultural process depicted in Figure 1 would vary in direct proportion to the type of technology used at that stage. Heichel [3] gives a revealing example of the effects of differing levels of technology on the quantity of energy consumed. Using the basic figures given by Heichel, Table II was developed to illustrate this fact.

Table II. Energy Budget and Savings to Produce a 100-Bu/ac Corn Crop Under Conventional and Minimum Tillage and Conventional and Manure Fertilization[a]

Tillage	Fertilizer	Energy Use Mcal/acre	Savings Mcal/acre
Conventional	Conventional	2925	
	Manures	2573	352
Minimum	Conventional	2753	172
	Manures	2401	524

[a]Adapted from Heichel [3].

Although definitive empirical evidence is lacking, it seems logical to conclude that, as a rule, capital-intensive technologies are also energy-intensive. Likewise, labor-intensive technologies tend to be less energy-intensive. In view of the diversity of technologies used in agriculture, energy-use coefficients derived from averages are of limited value. Energy researchers would, therefore, do well to specify the type or level of technology used at every stage of the production process in reporting energy consumption data.

Geographic Regions

Geography plays a dominant role in agriculture, and there are a number of ways in which energy use in agriculture can be reported on a geographic basis. These could be classified into two major categories: political and nonpolitical. The former would include national, state and county delineations. These are useful boundaries because most statistical data is collected and reported on this basis. The U.S. Department of Agriculture (USDA) production areas and state planning districts, among others, consist of an aggregation of smaller political units. The major disadvantage of this system stems from the fact that agriculture does not respect political boundaries. Agricultural production often transcends boundaries and is frequently more homogeneous across political boundaries than within. Most agricultural products are transported for processing and final consumption without regard to such artificial delineations.

Agroclimatic zones and river basins are examples of the nonpolitical geographic areas. The major advantage of this approach lies in the fact that it provides a more homogeneous and natural basis to report on agriculture. The smaller and more homogeneous the geographic region, the better the chances are for having accurate and useful information. Its limitation is that few primary data are currently available on a nonpolitical geographic basis. Hence, energy-use data will have to be obtained from other than available published sources.

Time

Because of the seasonal nature of agriculture, the time dimension assumes considerable importance in the allocation and consumption of energy. Many agricultural commodities are produced at specific times of the year, creating seasonal demands for energy all across the agricultural system. For example, most vegetables are produced for marketing and processing within a very short span of time, creating peak demands for energy.

For purposes of energy policy formulation and planning, it is imperative to have time-specific data. Consequently, reporting energy requirement data on a monthly or quarterly basis is much superior to reporting annual requirements. As a rule, the shorter the time period, the more useful will be the data.

CONCLUSIONS

This chapter has identified six dimensions which are of special importance in accurately determining the energy needs of agriculture. A uniform definition of the term "production" is essential to determine the energy requirements of different products on a comparable basis. The problem here is identifying a point in the production process which sets a base for the estimation of the total energy requirements. The complexities involved are demonstrated by the wheat example.

There is an overwhelming need for energy data disaggregation. The rule of thumb in this case is: the more detailed the information, the better. Such information is essential for intelligent analysis and interpretation of research results as a basis for sound and realistic energy policy formulation. The energy flow model developed in this chapter should prove to be useful in this connection, because it is aimed at the generation of specific information for the different stages of agricultural production and the activities within each stage.

The concept of "economic energy" and its further disaggregation into direct and indirect sources (the latter again subdivided into "ancillary" and "embodied" energy) should help refine the quality of energy data developed. There is a clear need for a common unit of measurement for reporting energy use data to replace the current bewildering array of units of measurement.

In the quest for ensuring uniformity and comparability of energy use data, the twin dimensions of space (geography) and time play a dominant role. The limitations have been pointed out of the traditional geographic classification based on political boundaries and the adoption of a new approach has been urged. The analysis also shows the importance of time-specific data in energy policy analysis.

There is a close connection between the amount of energy consumed in agriculture and the type of technology employed. Energy-use and requirements estimation, without taking into account the "technology differential," could prove to be misleading. We have shown that the specification of the type or level of technology used at every stage of the production process would enhance markedly the value of the data reported.

REFERENCES

1. Piementel, D. L. et al. "Food Production and the Energy Crisis," *Science* 183 (4111):443-449 (1973).
2. Heichel, G. H. "Comparative Efficiency of Energy Use in Crop Production," Bulletin 739, Connecticut Agricultural Experiment Station, New Haven (1974).
3. Heichel, G. H. "Agricultural Production and Energy Uses of Resources," *Am. Sci.* 64:64-72 (1976).
4. Slesser, M. "Energy Subsidy as a Criterion in Food Policy Planning," *J. Sci. Food Agric.* 24:1193-1207 (1973).
5. Hirst, E. "Energy Use for Food in the United States," Report No. 57, Oak Ridge National Laboratory, Oak Ridge, TN (1973).
6. "The U.S. Food and Fiber-Sector: Energy Outlook," U.S. Department of Agriculture, U.S. Government Printing Office (1974).
7. Steinhart, J. S. and C. E. Steinhart. "Energy Use in the U.S. Food System," *Science* 183 (4134):307-316 (1974).
8. Cervinka, V. et al. "Energy Requirements for Agriculture in California," Department of Food and Agriculture, University of California, Davis (1974).
9. Herendeen, R. A. "The Energy Costs of Goods and Services," Oak Ridge National Laboratory, Oak Ridge, TN (1973).

Part 2

CASE STUDIES

CHAPTER 5

WATER RESOURCE DEVELOPMENT—
SOME INSTITUTIONAL ASPECTS:
A CASE HISTORY OF MONTANA

INTRODUCTION

The rapidly increasing demand for water, coupled with its comparatively limited supply, has made it an "ocean-sized" problem in the United States in recent years. The situation is acute, especially in the chronically water-short western regions. The extent of the problem will become even clearer when the sharp rise in the demand for and use of water in the past few years is examined closely and related to the potential for increasing water supply. The demand for water for different uses has actually been increasing at a much faster pace than the increase in supply, particularly in the western United States. This imbalance in the supply-demand situation contains within itself the elements of a "coming water famine" which calls for the adoption of a series of corrective measures.

The strategic role of water in the development of arid and semiarid regions is perhaps nowhere more manifest than in the institutional factors governing its control and use. The purpose of this chapter is to focus attention on some of the institutional impediments related to Montana's water resource development and to indicate how these institutional aspects have considerably slowed the optimum development of the state's water resources.

THE LEGAL FRAMEWORK

In Montana the ownership, control and use of both surface and groundwater are governed by the doctrine of prior appropriation. Consequently, the system of water rights there suffers from some of the basic weaknesses of the appropriation doctrine: First, the system is inflexible. This stems from the freezing of rights in terms of the original appropriation. A certain degree of rigidity occurs if appropriation rights cannot be severed from the land on which the water is applied and are limited to the purpose for which it was originally diverted. This rigidity may result in economically or socially unsound water use. For example, the prior appropriation of much of the available water for irrigation hampers the reallocation of water to urban and industrial uses. Second, the heavy emphasis on priority often results in considerable waste. The conditions under which the original appropriation took place frequently change. Consequently, the water appropriated may no longer be needed in the amount, at the place or for the purpose specified, although the appropriator still continues to enjoy fully his right of use. Third, despite the doctrine of state administration, actual management is often vested with local water commissioners appointed either by county governing bodies or irrigation district boards, with the state official nominally responsible merely giving approval to the appointments. "This is not a particularly reliable process for bringing expertise to bear on a state program" [1].

More specifically, the following drawbacks have been pointed out in the Montana system of water rights:

1. The present system of appropriation by notice-posting and determination of rights by private suits, in which it is not necessary to join all parties concerned, is regarded as outdated. Where centralized systems exist, the supervision and control of the state is usually exercised through the state engineer or an administrative agency. The function of the courts in such cases is normally limited to deciding questions of priority of appropriation or appeals from administrative decisions. Montana has an administrative agency, the State Water Conservation Commis-

sion, and needs only to have the legislature broaden the scope of its activities. The office of state engineer has been abolished in Montana, and its duties have been transferred to the Montana Water Conservation Board.

A first step in this direction was taken in 1939, when the state engineer was empowered to sue for adjudication of streams. However, the system is still administered by water commissioners appointed by local courts, and records are required to be filed in the office of the clerk or the court concerned. Montana's primary need in the field of water law, according to legal experts, is a centralized system of administration designed to regulate the determination of existing rights, the distribution of water among those entitled to its use and the acquisition of new rights. Such an arrangement will be of considerable help in the transfer of water from a less-productive to a more-productive use and also from one user to another [2].

2. Montana rules specify that to constitute abandonment in that state there must be concurrence of relinquishment of possession, and intent not to resume it for a beneficial use. Most of the other western states have, however, provided by statute for forfeiture after a certain number of years, usually three to five. But there is no such provision in Montana law [2]. Viewed in a context of ever-increasing demand for water, this uncertainty would only contribute to a reduction in the efficiency and expediency of water use.

3. Montana law provides that:

> to ripen into a prescriptive title, there must be a continuous, exclusive, uninterrupted, notorious and adverse use of the water under claim of right throughout the statutory period, a result difficult to attain in a state where water flows in many streambeds only in certain months of the year. The problem may be further complicated sometimes by drouth which may prevent some streams from containing any water for years [2].

This indicates that to devise an efficient system of water administration within the state, it is essential to bring about substantial alterations in the existing provisions concerning prescription.

Stone points out that:

> Montana is limited in developing her water resources by laws and administrative patterns which were formed before Montana

became a state. No law enables Montana to develop multi-purpose projects, or to give recognition, and thereby lay the basis for a claim, to some of the uses of water which do not entail storage or diversion. Neither is the public interest represented in the development of new uses or applications of water in Montana [3].

CONSERVANCY DISTRICTS

An important institution which merits special consideration is the conservancy district. The question of conservancy districts has taken on a new importance in Montana not only because of its economic implications, but because of its somewhat intriguing political ramifications.

Although Montana does have a number of special districts to serve a variety of purposes, it does not have even a single conservancy district at present. What is more important is the fact that the state does not have even an enabling act which permits the establishment of conservancy districts.

Virtually all of these special districts are single-purpose in nature. A unique feature of the conservancy district that distinguishes it from other special districts is that it is essentially multipurpose in nature. The setting up of multipurpose conservancy districts in Montana is designed to conserve and develop Montana's water resources for flood protection, river control, drainage, water storage, irrigation, industrial and domestic use, waste disposal, pollution control, recreation and other beneficial purposes.

Several western states have already established conservancy districts. Conservancy districts were authorized by the Colorado legislature as far back as 1937. Colorado has the general enabling act type of legislation. At present Colorado has 32 conservancy districts. North Dakota formed the Garrison Diversion Conservancy District in 1955 by a special act of the state legislature. Montana is one of the few states in the West that does not have any provision for an enabling act to create Conservancy Districts.

All these districts have as their basic objective the multipurpose development of their water resources.

They supplement rather than replace other types of legal organizations that are established for water resource development such as irrigation districts and others. More and more the Conservancy District type of organization is being recognized as the answer to two of the perplexing problems encountered in the problems of today's more complicated water resources projects, namely (1) the financing of the local share of more costly projects being constructed today, and (2) providing the local administrative machinery through which the various interests in a multiple purpose water resources development can be represented [4].

There has been very limited state and local development of water resources in Montana in the course of the past ten years or so. A principal reason for this is the fact that single-purpose projects (such as those constructed by irrigation, drainage, county water, and soil and water conservation districts) do not permit adequate financing.

The justification for the development of more water resource projects now extends beyond the cultivation of crops on the irrigated lands. The creation of conservancy districts could result in a number of benefits like flood control; regulation of streams; improvement or reclamation of wetlands; recreation; conservation of water resources and related lands including fish and wildlife preserves; industrial development; municipal or domestic water supply; and the watering of livestock. It was this need for multipurpose approach toward water resource development at a local level that resulted in the demand for the establishment of conservancy districts.

There is a strong need for the creation of conservancy districts in Montana. Small water projects could be developed in Montana if it were possible to enlist the cooperation of all the beneficiaries involved. The easier-to-build and cheaper projects were first built in the state, chiefly as single-purpose projects.

A bill designed to create conservancy districts was introduced in the 1967 Montana State Legislature. The bill was passed by the Senate with an overwhelming majority—out of a total of 55 members, 46 voted in favor of it. However, the bill was defeated by the House, with 49 members voting against the bill and 46 members in favor of it.

The bill's defeat was attributed by knowledgeable circles to the "politics of water" in Montana. Some legislators have characterized the "killing" of the bill by the House "the high crime of the 40th Legislature." According to the "Great Falls Tribune," a widely circulated newspaper published in Montana, "the 40th Legislative Assembly may well be known as the session that pulled the plug on Montana's future water supply" [5].

In any case, the defeat of the conservancy district legislation points to the crucial role played by political factors in the overall institutional complex governing the water resource development of Montana.

ROLE OF STATE AGENCIES

A number of reforms are possible in the case of the state administrative agencies concerned with water development problems. In the first place, these agencies are handicapped by a severe dearth of funds. The state legislature does not appear to be in any hurry to grant appropriations in adequate amounts to enable the various state agencies to undertake water development activities within the state. Second, a pronounced lack of coordination exists between the activities of the various state and local groups engaged in water development. For example, it is well known that the State Water Conservation Board and the State Fish and Wild Life Commission often are not on particularly friendly terms. Third, some of the agencies are rather sluggish in implementing water development activities. Thus, the Montana Water Conservation Board had developed 181 small water-development projects by November, 1966 [6], the same number as it had developed at the end of June, 1960 [7]. In other words, over a period of more than six years the Board did not construct a single water conservation project.

The extreme reluctance on the part of the state government to allot funds for the conduct of water research has slackened the pace of urgently needed research. Adjoining states have already launched major programs to estimate their future needs. Huffman pointed out recently that Montana has not appropriated a single cent for the university-based Water Resources Research Center. In sharp contrast, Washington, Oregon and Idaho have appropriated large amounts to promote water resources research. For example, Washington is spending about $180,000 for an integrated study of water resources. Oregon is spending $743,000 for three different studies and Idaho, which created a Water Board as late as 1965, is providing over $125,000 for water resources research [8]. These figures should, if anything, act as an eye-opener to the Montana planners, and provision should be made in the future legislatures to appropriate a substantial amount for the conduct of comprehensive water planning and research. Time is running out and unless prompt measures are taken Montana may find itself deprived of a large part of its water by other downstream users who have established beneficial use of the state's waters.

ROLE OF FEDERAL GOVERNMENT

Another institutional factor closely related to the problem of water resource development concerns the attitude of the general public toward federal participation in water projects. Large numbers of citizens in Montana look down upon any form of federal involvement as detrimental to the well-being of the state. It is often argued, even by knowledgeable persons, that federal participation invariably leads to a curtailment of freedom on the part of the people of the state and deprives them of some of their cherished "rights and privileges." However, this type of argument is steadily losing ground and there is a rapidly increasing awareness of the role of federal government in the areas of state resource development.

Renne has indicated the strategic role of federal activities in the water resource development of Montana [9]. He refers in this connection to six major pieces of legislation passed by Congress in the past two years. Six of these which are likely to have a marked bearing on Montana's economy are: The Water Quality Act, the Solid Waste Disposal Act, the Land and Water Conservation Fund Act, the Federal Water Project

Recreation Act, the Water Resources Research Act and the Water Resources Planning Act. These six acts provide federal cooperation, technical assistance and funds to state and local governments by which major improvements can be effected.

A brief indication of the impact of the 1965 Water Resources Planning Act on the federal government programs will make this clear. Under the new federal law which provides financial assistance to states, Montana will receive about $100,000 a year on a matching 50-50 basis to carry on comprehensive planning of its water development [10].

The Water Resources Research Act makes available direct grant funds on a nonmatching basis for the establishment of research centers. These funds amount to $75,000 the first year, $85,000 the second year and $100,000 during subsequent years.

The most important recent development, perhaps, is the approval by the National Water Resources Council of the establishment of a regional water planning commission for five Pacific Northwest states, of which Montana is one [11]. The Water Resources Council which has approved the formation of this commission is also the result of the national Water Resources Planning Act.

CONSERVATION VS DAM BUILDING

In view of the potential importance of water-based recreation to Montana, a controversial aspect of recreation development has to be examined carefully. This relates to the long-standing controversy between preservationists and the federal agencies responsible for the construction of dams and reclamation of land (the Corps of Engineers and the Bureau of Reclamation). The feuds between these two groups have greatly slowed down the tempo of water resources development.

The extreme view held by some conservationists that all dam construction is detrimental and potentially damaging to wilderness, wildlife and scenic beauty is certainly untenable.

The fact is that most of the dams and reclamation projects do contribute to the development of the environment.

Reclamation, in storing the spring runoff and regulating our streams for the public benefit is not the great destroyer, but in fact consistently improves the rivers for all purposes including recreational uses and enjoyment of natural beauty [12].

The majestic scenery surrounding Lake Mead (Nevada) and Lake Powell (Arizona)—both Bureau of Reclamation lakes—give support to this view.

However, the view held by some building agencies that the enjoyment and pleasure derived from viewing beautiful scenery, wilderness areas or wild rivers are only of secondary importance if they do not contribute any tangible earnings is not justifiable. To quote Robinson, the British economist:

> The fight that has to be put up, for instance, to keep wild country from being exploited for money profit is made more difficult because its defenders can be represented as standing up for "non-economic" values (which is considered soft-headed, foolish and unpatriotic) though the economist should have been the first to point out that *utility*, not money, is economic value and that the utility of goods is not measured by their prices [13].

Viewed in this perspective, the idea of preserving stretches of certain rivers as wild rivers can be justified in economic terms. Hence, the argument against the selection of stretches of the Flathead and upper Missouri Rivers to be included in a national system of wild rivers on the ground that they do not make any contribution of economic value loses strength.

These, then, are some of the institutional blocks in addition to legal handicaps which slow down the tempo of Montana's efforts to maximize the efficiency of its water use. A determined effort on the part of enlightened Montanans to remove these institutional bottlenecks should contribute immensely to the state's water development.

CONCLUSIONS

The success of a program of water resource development thus depends not merely on economic considerations but on a host of institutional factors as well. The search for efficiency in water utilization through water transfer can be successful only if these institutional aspects are reckoned with. In order to overcome most of the major institutional blocks—in addition to removing the legal and administrative handicaps—concerted efforts should be undertaken to educate people at the "grass roots" level. The results of technical research have to be passed on to the general public in a form that is fully comprehensible to them.

REFERENCES

1. Martin, R. C. *Water for New York* (Syracuse, NY: Syracuse University, 1960), p. 112.
2. Heman, H. W. "Irrigation Law," *Montana Law Rev.* 10:13 (1949), p. 13.
3. Stone, A. W. "Problems Arising out of Montana's Law of Water Rights," *Montana Law Rev.* 27(1):1 (1965).
4. Garrison Conservancy District "The Garrison Conservancy District." Unpublished.
5. Editorial, *Great Falls Tribune* (March 6, 1967).
6. *Summary of the Activities from Inception on January 22, 1934 to June 30, 1960* (Helena, MT: Montana State Water Conservation Board, 1961).
7. *Bozeman Chronicle*, November 18, 1966.
8. Huffman, R., Interview in the *Billings Gazette*, February 18, 1966; *Irrigation Development and Public Water Policy* (New York: Ronald Press, 1953).
9. Renne, R. R. Address in Bozeman, Mont., reported in the *Bozeman Chronicle*, February 18, 1967.
10. Huffman, R. Speech reported in *Bozeman Chronicle*, February 18, 1967.
11. *Bozeman Chronicle*, November 18, 1966.
12. Dominy, F. E. *Bozeman Chronicle*, November 17, 1966.
13. Robinson, J. *Economic Philosophy* (Chicago, IL: Aldine Publishing House, 1963), pp. 131–132.

CHAPTER 6

ECONOMIC GROWTH THROUGH
WATER RESOURCE DEVELOPMENT: INDIA

INTRODUCTION

The role of water resources in stimulating economic growth has begun to engage the serious attention of economic planners in developing countries. This is evidenced by the pride of place accorded to water development programs in their planning efforts. Investment in water resource projects during the last two decades has increased progressively in virtually all the developing nations and it currently accounts for a significant share of total plan outlays. This resurgence of interest in water resource planning is largely the result of two factors: the prospects for high economic and social returns, and the latent possibility that it might open up new avenues of economic development. Despite the growing recognition of the crucial role of water in the development process, only very few empirical studies exist in this area.

This chapter attempts to study the impact of India's multidimensional water development programs on the pace and pattern of its economic growth. First, the goals, objectives and philosophy underlying water development planning in India are discussed. Second, the actual progress achieved during the past two decades is briefly outlined, and the impact of India's massive water programs on the economy is analyzed in terms of several indices of economic growth. Third, specific areas of weakness in the country's water planning efforts are identified, and some suggestions for improvement are offered. Fourth, the critical role of the institutional structure in India's water development is reviewed in terms of selected institutional constraints, and the strategy for revamping it is explored.

DEVELOPING INDIA'S WATER RESOURCES: OBJECTIVES

The basic philosophy underlying water resource planning in India is that the rapid development of irrigation and power is essential for rejuvenating the country's predominantly agrarian economy and for facilitating its industrialization. From the start of the First Five Year Plan in 1951, Indian planners recognized the importance of water development in stimulating economic growth. The massive investments in India's Five Year Plans for the development of the nation's water potential have to be viewed in this perspective.

Irrigation and power have been among the most significant fields of development since the beginning of the First Plan (1951). Expansion of irrigation, from large as well as small projects, is an essential condition for diversifying agriculture and increasing crop yields. The development of power is a prerequisite for carrying out large industrial programs. . . . Thus, large-scale development of irrigation and power helps to rebuild the agricultural economy and to pave the way for the rapid industrialization of the country [1].

The Fourth Five Year Plan (1969-1974) categorically states: "The expansion of irrigation facilities in order to ensure timely and adequate water supply has thus, ever since the inception of planning, been an extremely important means of bringing about agricultural development" [2].

More specifically, the strategy for the development of the nation's water resources is designed to accomplish the following goals and objectives:

1. significant expansion in the ratio of irrigated area to total area under cultivation;
2. provision of irrigation water in adequate quantities and at appropriate times to expedite the "green revolution";
3. integrated use and efficient management of both surface and groundwater;
4. substantial increase in hydropower generation;
5. rural electrification with the focus on the pumpset (for irrigation and drinking water) rather than on domestic lighting; and
6. pollution abatement and water quality maintenance.

In water development, the Fourth Plan differs from the previous plans in two important respects. First, during the Fourth Plan there has been a clear shift in emphasis in the pattern of water resource use. Most of the existing projects are designed for single-crop irrigation and protection against failure of rain rather than to maximize agricultural production. The new policy puts the emphasis on optimizing production from irrigated lands and also on ensuring maximum efficiency in water use. This is to be carried out through changes in location and design of future works as well as the speedy construction of field channels and drainage facilities.

Second, the minor irrigation program received a distinct boost over the multipurpose projects. From a mere 20% of the total outlay on irrigation during the Second Plan, the outlay on minor irrigation went up to 32% during the Fourth Plan.

IMPACT OF WATER DEVELOPMENT
ON INDIAN ECONOMY

The impact of water development, both direct and indirect, on India's economy during the last two decades has been quite impressive. According to the latest estimates, India's total water potential is 78 million ha-m (56 million ha-m of surface water and 22 million ha-m of groundwater). Out of this, at the beginning of the First Five Year Plan in 1951, only 21% was being used. However, in 1969, as a result of concerted efforts, the actual use doubled, to 40% of total usable flow. The area under irrigation increased sharply from 22.6 to 35.9 million ha during the same period (1951–1969); no small accomplishment in a country where agriculture up until recently was a "gamble in the rains" (Table I).

The Planning Commission estimates that 82 million ha can be ultimately irrigated from combined surface and groundwater sources. At the beginning of the First Plan, the total potential stood at 27.6% of the ultimate potential. In 1969, it increased to 45.7%.

Table II gives information pertaining to expenditures on minor, medium and major irrigation schemes for the four Five Year Plans. Irrigation was given a pivotal role in the First Plan as is clear from the fact that more than 16% of its total outlay was for irrigation alone. This constituted a slightly higher amount than the total allotted to all other aspects of agriculture combined.

> Irrigation received major emphasis in the First Plan because water plays such an important role in Indian agriculture and because the types of administrative and capital resources were abundant at the time the First Plan was framed. Under Indian climatic conditions, irrigation benefits the farmer by greatly lessening risk in growing a crop and by increasing the average yields [5].

Table I. Development of Irrigation Potential, 1950–1969 [1-4]

Period	Potential[a] $(10^6$ ha$)$[b]
1950–1951	22.6 (27.6)[c]
1960–1961	29.2 (35.6)
1968–1969	37.5 (45.7)

[a]Ultimate water potential is estimated to be 82 million ha.
[b]One hectare = 2.47 ac.
[c]Figures in parentheses represent potential created as percentage of the ultimate potential.

Table II. Outlay on Minor, Medium and Major Irrigation Schemes, 1951–1974 [14]

Type of Irrigation	First Plan 1951–1956		Second Plan 1956–1961		Third Plan 1961–1966		Fourth Plan 1969–1974	
	Amount (Rupees Crores)[a]	Percent Total Outlay	Amount (Rupees Crores)	Percent Total Outlay	Amount (Rupees Crores)	Percent Total Outlay	Amount (Rupees Crores)	Percent Total Outlay
Minor Irrigation[b]	NA[c]		95	20	177	23	516	32
Medium[d] and Major[e]	300		372	80	600	77	954	68
Total	NA		467	100	777	100	1589	100

[a]The term crore signifies 10,000,000. One crore of rupees (Rs.) at the current exchange rate equals $1.3 million.
[b]Costing Rs. 1.5 million or less.
[c]NA Not available.
[d]Costing more than Rs. 1.5 million but not above Rs. 50 million.
[e]Costing more than Rs. 50 million.

Although the Second and Third Plans were primarily industry-oriented, irrigation continued to enjoy a special place in the planning process. The total outlay on irrigation more than doubled during the Fourth Plan as compared to the Third Plan. This, in part, is caused by the sharp increase in the overall outlay; but to a large extent, it reflects the progressively expanding role of irrigation, especially minor irrigation (Table II).

Minor Irrigation

Minor irrigation has been steadily gaining importance as a significant source of water supply to India's parched agricultural lands. It consists of groundwater schemes and those surface water schemes which are estimated to cost up to Rs. 1.5 million. The Fourth Plan is contemplating revision of this figure to Rs. 3 million. Minor irrigation consists of well irrigation, tube-wells, tanks, reservoirs, diversion weirs and small irrigation channels, and is primarily the responsibility of the state.

The comparative advantages of minor irrigation over other forms of irrigation have been summed up by a Planning Commission Report:

> . . . minor irrigation works have a comparatively short gestation period. . . . Secondly, these works can be executed with the help of local resources and equipment. Thirdly, the foreign exchange component of such schemes is very little or nil. Fourthly, these works provide a large amount of dispersed employment. . . . Both local employment as well as people's participation can, therefore, be counted upon for the construction of such works. Lastly, the commitment of the Government by way of expenditure is relatively small because a fairly high proportion of these works is either privately owned or owned by local groups or bodies [1].

Over the years the tube-wells have come to play a dominant role in minor irrigation. The deep tube-wells, by and large, are community-based; open wells and shallow tube-wells are mostly privately built and owned. "In either case, the ground water provides the farmer with just the type of instant and controlled irrigation which the new high-yielding varieties of seed demand" [2].

The anticipated benefits from minor irrigation under the Fourth Plan are given in Table III. Thus, the total area benefiting from minor irrigation schemes is expected to be 5.6 million ha, compared to 4.2 million ha during the period 1961–1969.

The total outlay on minor irrigation under the Fourth Plan is approximately Rs. 516 crores. The investments will be made by the public sector, financial institutions and private sector. Some significant new trends in minor irrigation are reduction of subsidies, stress on state or community works to assist the small farmer, larger provision of institutional finance and the establishment of agencies to survey and develop groundwater schemes. Also, special emphasis is being placed on the proper upkeep of pumping machinery and irrigation tanks.

Flood Control

Indian villages from time immemorial have been subjected to large-scale floods, especially in the wake of the monsoons, just as they have been ravaged by frequent droughts, both of which have made agriculture an enormously risky and uncertain proposition. The Fourth Plan fully recognizes the need to reduce the flood hazards as far as possible. During 1953–1968, floods affected annually an average of 6 million ha, of which the cultivated area was about 2 million ha. The Fourth Plan hopes

Table III. Benefits from Minor Irrigation, 1969–1974 [1-4]

Source	Benefits (10^6 ha)
New Irrigation Added	4.80
Depreciation on Existing Works	1.60
Net New Irrigated Area	3.20
Benefit from Improved Irrigation Supplies	2.25
Benefits from Drainage and Embankments	0.15

to protect a total of 16 million ha liable to floods. The principal components of the program are: an integrated scheme of flood control, drainage, antiwaterlogging works and the establishment of a scientific flood forecasting system. The Fourth Plan has earmarked Rs. 133 crores for flood control programs (Table IV).

Soil Conservation

Erosion, waterlogging, salinity and drainage have been major problems with which Indian agriculturists have always had to contend. The Fourth Plan has developed an "area saturation" approach to treat different types of land on a complete-watershed basis. Virtually all the states have enacted legislation for soil and water conservation. Top priority will be given to increasing storage reservoirs for irrigation and power generation.

Rural Electrification

Rural electrification has been one of the central concerns of Indian planners from the inception of the First Five Year Plan, because more than 80% of the country's population lives in villages, which total over 5 million, scattered all over the country. In 1950, before commencement of the First Plan,

Table IV. Third (1961–1966) and Fourth (1969–1974) Plan Outlays on Irrigation and Related Services (Rupees Crores) [1–4]

Service	Outlay		
	Third Plan	Fourth Plan	% Increase
Irrigation (Major and Medium)	583.2	953.8	64
Irrigation (Minor)	270.1	515.7	91
Rural Electrification	105.0	444.7	324
Flood Control	81.5	132.7	63
Soil Conservation	77.0	159.4	107

only 3623 villages (0.6%) were electrified. In 1970, the corresponding figure stood at 85,859 (15.1%)—a phenomenal increase (Table V). The tempo of rural electrification gained considerable momentum during the First and Second Plan periods, and actually overshot the target at the end of the Third Plan.

Until the end of the Third Plan, the focus of rural electrification was on domestic lighting. However, the acute food shortage India experienced during 1965 and 1966 led to a reorientation of the program, emphasizing provision of energy to irrigation pumpsets and tube-wells with a view to increase agricultural production (Table VI).

Because of India's unique characteristics, rural electrification has to be viewed as a social service rather than a purely economic activity, the main components of which are: irrigation pumping, agricultural processing industries, drinking water and street lighting. The domestic lighting load in most instances is negligible. The revenue derived often falls short of a minimum return on the investment in transmission lines, transformers and generators.

Table V. Progress of Rural Electrification, 1950–1970 [1-4]

Year	No. of Villages Electrified[a]	Percent of Total Villages
1950	3,623	0.6
1956	7,400	1.3
1961	25,630	4.5
1966	43,670	7.7
1970	85,859	15.1

[a]Total number of villages in India = 567,338.

Table VI. Number of Pumpsets, 1961–1974 [1-4]

Year	Pumpsets (thousands)
1961	192
1969 (est.)	1088
1974 (est.)	2337

As Robinson [6] rightly points out:

> The contribution of rural electrification is much more intangible and non-economic: a matter of welfare and of a psychological feeling that the rural areas as well as the great cities are benefiting from the modernization of the economy.

Viewed in light of this, the importance attached to rural electrification in the Five Year Plans seems entirely justifiable, especially because the country is planning for the creation of a welfare state.

A comparison of the Third and Fourth Plan outlays on irrigation (major, medium and minor), rural electrification, flood control and soil conservation is given in Table IV.

Hydropower Generation

The contribution of hydropower to India's ever-increasing energy requirements has registered significant progress in the course of the last decade. Both the installed capacity of and the power generated by the hydropower plants more than doubled during this period. In 1969, the hydropower plants accounted for 41% of the total installed capacity (which includes thermal and diesel, besides hydropower) and 44% of the energy generated (Table VII).

Table VII. Hydropower Generation, 1960-1969 [1-4]

	1960–1961	1965–1966	1968–1969
Installed Capacity (10^6 kW)	1.92 (34)[a]	4.10 (40)	5.91 (41)
Energy Generated (10^6 kWh)	6,837 (46)	15,225 (46)	20,744 (44)

[a]Figures in parentheses express hydropower as a percent of the total from all sources—thermal, diesel and hydropower.

Power potential studies of the river basins of India indicate an aggregate hydropower potential of 41.1 million kW at 60% load factor, of which only about 6 million kW has been tapped. Thus, there is considerable untapped potential to draw on in the years ahead to meet the burgeoning demands of industrialization, rural electrification and the rapidly expanding population.

ROLE OF WATER IN THE "GREEN REVOLUTION"

The importance of water resource development in promoting India's economic growth is perhaps nowhere more manifest than in the key role it plays in the context of the so-called "green revolution." Brown draws pointed attention to this:

> The new seeds are generating an enormous thirst for irrigation water among millions of farmers in the poor countries where they are being introduced. For many, water has suddenly become the key to a better life. With an adequate supply of water, farmers can use the new wheats or rices, raise their living standards, and enter the twentieth century; without it, they remain tied to traditional agriculture, merely eking out a subsistence living [7].

Thus, irrigation has taken on a new importance, because the success of the green revolution depends to a pronounced degree on the availability of assured water supplies, in the right amounts and at the right times.

The green revolution consequently has led to the formulation of new irrigation strategies.

> Tube wells (closed cylindrical shafts driven into the ground) and electric pumps have suddenly become popular with farmers. Accordingly, governments have put more emphasis on encouraging small scale irrigation that farmers can install in a matter of days or weeks rather than on huge irrigation systems that take many years and millions of dollars to construct [7].

This shift in emphasis, as pointed out earlier, is clearly reflected in the sharp increase in outlay on minor irrigation in the Fourth Plan.

The Fourth Plan recognizes the crucial role of water in realizing the full potential of the high-yielding seeds. Controlled irrigation is essential for the supply of water at critical periods of plant growth.

> Experiments already made show that four irrigations applied at crown root, flowering, milk, and dough stages of development are as efficient in terms of yield as six irrigations applied indiscriminately. This irrigation efficiency which is basic to the success of high yielding varieties program has to be developed as part of the requisite cultural practices [2].

The proportion of land that can be brought under irrigation sets a limit to the rate of growth in agricultural production that can be effected by technological change. The Fourth Plan has, no doubt, acknowledged the crucial interrelation between water and the new seed varieties. However, a more dynamic role has to be accorded to irrigation because the technological revolution that is sweeping over Indian agriculture relies very heavily on assured water supplies.

Also, it is significant to note that the new seeds resulted in increased agricultural production only when adequate amounts of complementary inputs of fertilizers and other plant nutrients were used, besides guaranteed water supplies. Hence, measures have to be implemented to make available complementary inputs in addition to irrigation water to ensure the success of the green revolution.

EMPLOYMENT POTENTIAL

The development of water resources contributes to India's economic growth by the provision of substantial employment opportunities through the initiation of a large number of labor-intensive irrigation and multipurpose projects.

From the outset, special attention has been given to the use of the local labor force in the construction of mammoth multipurpose projects. This is clearly illustrated by Nagarjunasagar Dam, the world's largest masonry dam, which was built mainly by manual labor, using minimum machinery. During peak periods, as many as 50,000 people worked in various types of construction activity associated with the project.

The project labor force consisted mainly of local workers. Also, labor from surrounding areas was brought in to meet the growing needs. Mechanics, drivers, blacksmiths, carpenters, masons and other artisans were recruited through an employment exchange at the dam site [8]. The labor force employed during the construction of the dam is shown in Figure 1.

The Fourth Plan focuses special attention on the labor content of the major, medium and minor irrigation and flood control schemes proposed for implementation during the plan period. These are expected to generate steadily rising employment opportunities apart from underemployment relief in the rural areas. The minor irrigation works are likely to prove especially beneficial to the small farmers. In addition programs of flood control, drainage and antiwaterlogging are expected to provide plenty of employment opportunities to skilled and semiskilled workers, in addition to employing civil engineers and other highly trained technical personnel.

The green revolution apparently has been instrumental in creating significant employment opportunities through increased demand for irrigation water—an aspect that has received scant attention. According to a recent study:

> The new seeds have created a vast new demand for irrigation pumps and tube wells. In 1956, there were 27 firms in India manufacturing this equipment, with a total annual capacity of 67,000 pumps. In 1966, some 200,000 were produced. Meeting the estimated demand for 400,000 pumps in 1970 should mean the employment of close to a quarter of a million laborers in the production of the steel used in the pumps and in the manufacture and distribution [7].

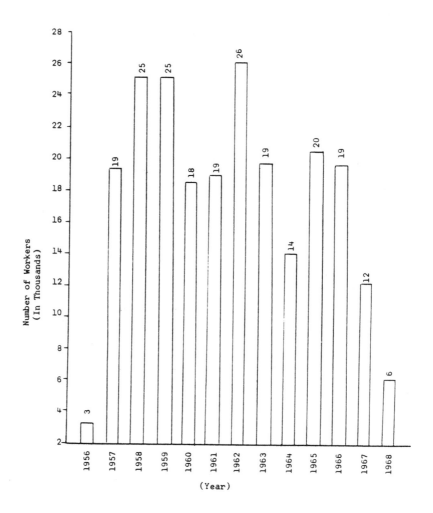

Figure 1. Labor force at Nagarjunasagar Dam, 1956–1968 [8].

Selective mechanization in using the new seeds can also produce new employment. Irrigation is an instance in point. In
many cases, traditional irrigation practices cannot cope with
the increasing water requirements of the high-yielding seeds.
Hence, pumps are being used progressively, which make water

available in sufficient quantities, thereby significantly increasing the labor demand for land preparation, planting, fertilizing, weeding, harvesting and threshing. Also, multiple cropping may lead to a doubling or even tripling of the labor requirements. Thus, both selective mechanization and intensive cropping create new jobs. However, to realize fully the employment potential of the green revolution, a wide range of price, investment, tax, credit and import policies have to be judiciously orchestrated.

INDIA'S WATER PLANNING
A CRITICAL APPRAISAL

Despite the marked progress India has made in developing its water resources, thereby contributing to the country's economic growth, its water planning strategy leaves much room for improvement. This section attempts to identify some of the more serious weaknesses that have characterized India's water planning efforts and to point to the need for modifying some of the current practices.

Estimation of Indirect Benefits

Despite the importance accorded to water resource development, no serious attention has been given to the formulation of rational and meaningful criteria and empirical bases for the choice of new water development (either irrigation or multiple purpose) projects. One of the major areas of weakness relates to the determination of indirect benefits from water development. Indirect benefits refer to the benefits which accrue indirectly to the farm and nonfarm sectors of the economy. These benefits can be further divided into two categories—benefits "stemming from" and "induced by" the project. Increase in income and employment from the processing of the immediate products falls under the first category; the second category consists of those benefits which accrue because of the increased expenditure on goods and services by the producers of the immediate products [9].

The indirect benefits from irrigation development, according to empirical studies conducted in the United States and in other developed economies, often account for more than 50% of the total benefits [10]. These indirect benefits or "side effects" are much more pronounced in the developing countries and "must be closely watched and capitalized" [11]. The same view is shared by Bruton [12]. He points out that in addition to the direct effects, "there are other effects that are of consequence to the development process, and hence of relevance to the allocation problem." Tinbergen also emphasizes the need for taking into account what he calls the "secondary consequences" from development projects in the case of developing countries [13].

The financial return of a development project to the exclusion of other considerations is consequently an especially unsatisfactory guide to investment decisions in developing countries.

> The essential point is that there is apt to be considerable divergence in an under-developed economy between private and social returns. The financial yield on invested capital measures only the former, and hence it is an inadequate, even misleading criterion to go by in investment decisions. It follows that if any other criterion, or set of criteria, is to be more adequate from this point of view, it must provide a reasonably good measure of the social returns from particular investments [14].

Economists, on the whole, agree that the indirect benefits unleashed by a development project tend to be quite significant in a developing economy. It is true that several of the indirect benefits of irrigation cannot be expressed in precise, quantitative terms. However, the principal indirect benefits that should be taken into account include: (1) more intensive use of land and other resources; (2) adoption of a better cropping pattern and a shift to more valuable crops; (3) creation of conditions favorable to productive investment in farm business;

(4) increased employment opportunities for labor; and (5) stimulus to industry, especially the processing industry, trade and transport. Thus, the indirect benefits are central to the building of a strong infrastructure conducive to overall economic development.

Despite the significance of indirect benefits, a good deal of planning effort in the area of water development has ignored this aspect or relegated it to the background. Formulation of more meaningful and realistic cost-benefit ratios incorporating the full gamut of indirect or secondary benefits, therefore, deserves special priority in the future planning of water projects in India. There must be growing awareness that development projects are undertaken on the basis of net social benefits and not on net financial returns to the government.

Underutilization

In planning the development of India's water potential, adequate attention has not been paid to the provision of facilities to ensure its full use. As a result, underutilization of water potential has always existed. The main reasons for the pronounced gap between created potential and the actual use seem to be the fixing of unrealistic (too high) targets and the sharp rise in the actual costs of several projects. Thus, at the end of the First Plan (March 1956), only 48% of the potential was used. Inadequate local financing and marked foreign exchange shortage have also resulted in shortfalls in some instances. The other causes for uderutilization are:

1. lag in the excavation of field channels;
2. lack of land preparation;
3. lack of adequate research information;
4. ignorance of farmers in regard to the requirements of irrigated farming [15].

It is to be mentioned, however, that the planners have been able to accomplish progressively significant reductions in underutilization over the last two decades. Thus, the Second and the Third Plans witnessed sharp rises in use, 73 and 78%, respectively, with the Fourth Plan shooting for a 94% use.

Hirschman makes an interesting observation concerning the use of irrigation potential:

> In irrigation the road to full utilization often requires the solving of organizational problems and of technological uncertainty about the crops it is possible to grow and the removal of market uncertainty with respect to the crops. Utilization is, therefore, a matter of administrative, technological, and market problem solving that must be engaged in after the irrigation structures are in place, than of the simple picking up of clearly existing profitable opportunities by entrepreneurs who become gradually aware of them [11].

Rising Cost of Irrigation

Another disquieting feature of India's water planning has manifested itself in a progressive increase in the cost of irrigating an acre of land through major and medium irrigation projects during the three plan periods (1951–1966).

Table VIII shows that providing irrigation for an acre of land is becoming an increasingly expensive proposition. The reasons for a nearly twofold rise in the cost of creating irrigation potential per acre over a 15-year period can be identified only when individual cost components are carefully analyzed. Some of the possible reasons are: (1) inflationary cost-push; (2) administrative bottlenecks and the consequent delays in project execution; and (3) choice of inferior project sites—partly because of extra-economic considerations [16].

INSTITUTIONAL CONSTRAINTS

Institutional factors are an aspect of water resource development in developing countries that has received very little attention from economists and planners. A good deal of the responsi-

Table VIII. Cost Per Acre of Irrigation Potential [16]

	I Plan	II Plan	III Plan	Overall
Expenditure (Rs. Crores)[a]	380.00	375.85	603.15[b]	1359.0
Irrigation Potential (Crores of Acres)	0.647	0.562	0.591	1.800
Per Acre Cost of Irrigation Potential (Rs.)	587.33	668.77	1020.56	755.0

[a]One crore of rupees, at the current exchange rate, equals $1.3 million.
[b]Third Plan figures are provisional.

bility for the failure to use fully the available opportunities must be placed on the inherited institutional system. Farmers are often extremely reluctant to use water placed at their disposal and, in particular, to shift to double cropping. They frown on any disruptions in their accustomed rhythm of life, and there is often economic justification for this attitude in the prevailing rural structure.

One such reason is that the landlord, the water authorities, and hired laborers all insist on the same rate of payment for the second planting as for the first, though the second usually yields less and requires more. Sharecroppers, particularly, may be reluctant to commit themselves to a pattern of operations dependent on irrigation water when they fear that in a drought the requirements of those higher in the rural power structure will be met and their own water ration cut off [17].

The impact of the institutional system can be best described in terms of specific instances. An especially graphic account of one such instance is given by Nair

And so it is that in this proverbially parched and thirsty land another crop of jowar is under harvest and women sit by the roadside tying the sheaves to load the bullock carts. Yet the area actually irrigated lags far behind the area that has been made irrigable and more than two-thirds of the water continues to run waste.

"After all, we have been growing our crops like this with only rain water for thousands of years," is the normal reply, accompanied by a shrug of the shoulder. And then the rain is free, while for the canal water they will have to pay once they agree to take it, irrespective of whether they use it or not. The peasant here is obviously not interested in increasing his productivity, which irrigation makes possible, but looks upon the latter simply as insurance against drought. For irrigation by itself will not give the maximum increase in crop yields, but only a more scientific technique of cultivation combined with the use of fertilizer and irrigation.

By the present method, on the other hand, the jowar grows almost by itself. The farmer simply broadcasts the seed after superficial ploughing and then returns only to harvest it. It involves no investment such as the new method requires—of using fertilizers, doing interculture and letting in water at regular intervals. And since there is plenty of land here, even at the rate of one or two bags an acre, the yield is sufficient to feed the family and often to enable it to tide over an intervening year of drought as well.

That is not all. These peasants are such brave and cheerful optimists that, despite the many droughts and famines they have had to face so often, they have not even bothered to sink any wells . . . [18].

The village to which Nair alludes is in Mysore in South India and to a certain extent typifies the attitude of the average Indian farmer.

And elsewhere, even when the farmers at the grassroots level are eager and willing to avail themselves of irrigation water, an institutional problem of a sharply contrasting nature arises, which makes the actual use of water well-nigh impossible for them. Such a situation exists in the Sarda Canal area of Uttar Pradesh in North India.

Throughout the Sarda system it is the general rule—there are of course some exceptions—that the strong, the powerful, the well-connected, the local *Zabardast* (bullies, etc.) dominate the use of irrigation water. They get water first and they tend to use as much of it as they please. Only after they are satisfied do they permit the mass of ordinary, unimportant, petty cultivators (the *kamzor log*) to have access to it.

The ordinary peasants of Sarda complain that the irrigation department is slow to provide canal water; the irrigation department complains that the ordinary peasants are generally slow to take canal water. The mass simply do not show the benefits that one would expect from regular irrigation, their appearance and the appearance of their villages help to confirm the impression that in the years since Sarda was founded in 1928 the ordinary peasants do not seem to have received the cumulative benefits of irrigation. . . . Thus, in the distribution of canal water the rule of the "strong" goes virtually unchallenged [19].

Further, the lack of a well-defined body of water laws in India to govern the ownership, control and appropriation of water adds to the hardships of the water users, especially the farmers at the grassroots level. Most states simply do not have any statutory regulations that control water use, and even where water laws exist, they are archaic and have outlived their utility. In any case, water laws have seldom been invoked in the settlement of water disputes. There is, therefore, a definite need to evolve meaningful water laws capable of effective implementation to meet the changing and challenging water requirements of the country.

The essential fact facing the nation is thus an immense contrast between the technical possibilities which irrigation holds out for a bright future and the human and institutional constraints leading to increasing difficulties. The primary problem therefore is one of finding ways to bridge this gap and to energize a stagnant rural sector with its deteriorating land and rising population. It is not so much a problem of discovery as of organization and implementation; the overwhelming need is not to provide advice, but to get "agriculture moving." There is thus an imperative need for more effective planning and management. As Myrdal explains it:

The dichotomy between ideals and reality, and even between enacted legislation and implementation should be seen against the background that India, like the other South Asian countries, is a soft state. There is an unwillingness among the rulers to impose obligations on the governed and a corresponding unwillingness on their part to obey rules laid down by the democratic process [17].

The high cost of providing additional water necessitates speedy improvement in yield. Technically, the decisive factor in increasing yield significantly is to use a combination or package of inputs which would serve as an inducement to the farmer to take extra risk and effort. Concentration on one input, water, alone is not sufficient; attention should be paid to the interlocking nature of all relevant inputs. As Gaitskell puts it:

Timely and ample water, properly levelled and prepared land, good quality seed tolerant to high fertilizer application, fertilizer, and lastly pest control—all these must be combined for the full impact to be gained in yield. Nor is this all. Credit, to get out of moneylenders' clutches, improved marketing, and a satisfactory price versus cost of inputs ratio, have to be an integral part of the interlocking chain if the farmers' incentive is to be aroused and his income raised [17].

Hence there is need for a package deal covering all these aspects in a perspective plan.

To gain new insights into the human dimensions of economic development is perhaps most important. Very few attempts have been made to explore the human factor in the development process, and in the absence of a body of reliable knowledge on this aspect, planning for water development will at best be an exercise in futility. Knowledge of the technical and economic aspects of water planning has to be combined with the knowledge of the psychological and motivational factors of the potential water users to evolve and implement an effective water policy. The resistance of farmers to the use of irrigation water, for instance, cannot be dismissed as yet another instance of apathy, fatalism or just plain laziness; the deeper meanings of resistance to change the familiar lifestyles have to be probed and researched thoroughly, and the new knowledge acquired in the process has to be incorporated into the macromodel of the water planner.

CONCLUSIONS

The experience of India in developing its water potential more or less corresponds to the experience of a number of developing countries, especially in Asia, and hence the observations made in this chapter have a large measure of general applicability. The reason for studying India's water planning strategy is not to recommend it in its entirety to other countries, but to point out the numerous less developed countries now genuinely striving for water development what complexities and blind alleys in planning and administering a viable and effective water policy might lie ahead of them, and, hopefully, to help them avoid these pitfalls. The Indian experience, more than anything else, brings into bold relief the need for adaptation of policies and institutions to meet and respond to the dynamics of social change.

Notwithstanding the shortcomings in its planning strategy, India provides a good example of a developing country whose economic growth has been influenced in a pronounced fashion by the development of its fairly substantial water potential. Progressively rising use of the created water potential has been contributing significantly to meet the country's everincreasing food requirements. Large increases in hydropower generation, besides accelerating the tempo of industrialization, have brought new life and light to India's myriad villages and have altered traditional lifestyles. Water development projects have served as successful catalysts in transforming surplus labor, especially in the countryside, as a source of capital formation, because of the shift in emphasis from capital-intensive, multipurpose projects to small-scale, labor-intensive schemes. The per capita income of the average farmer has stabilized, and in many cases, has actually gone up. The phenomenal success of the green revolution can be attributed in a large measure to the availability of assured water supplies. It has brought a new kind of security to hundreds of thousands of villagers by freeing them from the capricious outbursts of nature in the form of massive inundations or devastating droughts. Water development has thus permeated virtually every facet of India's overwhelmingly agrarian economy. From the arid "dust-bowls" of the Indian countryside a new life is blossoming. Water development has brought in its wake not only the green revolution, but the greening of India.

REFERENCES

1. Planning Commission of India. *Third Five Year Plan Report* (New Delhi: Government of India Press, 1961).
2. Planning Commission of India. *Fourth Five Year Plan Report* (New Delhi: Government of India Press, 1970).
3. Planning Commission of India. *Second Five Year Plan Report* (New Delhi: Government of India Press, 1956).
4. Planning Commission of India. *First Five Year Plan Report* (New Delhi: Government of India Press, 1952).
5. Mellor, J. W. et al. *Developing Rural India* (Ithaca, NY: Cornell University Press, 1968).
6. Robinson, E. A. G. "The Case of Energy Investment," in *The Crisis of Indian Planning*, P. Streeten and M. Lipton, Eds. (New York: Oxford University Press, Inc., 1968).
7. Brown, L. *Seeds of Change* (New York: Praeger Publishers, 1970).
8. Rao, B., and M. R. S. Somayajulu. *Bhagirath* XVI:43-46 (1963).
9. Wantrup, C. S. V. "Benefit-Cost Analysis in Public Resource Development," *J. Farm Econ.* 40:303-314 (1965).
10. Stewart, C. E. "Economic Evaluation of Public Irrigation Development," in *Economics and Public Policy in Water Resources Development*, S. C. Smith and E. N. Castle, Eds. (Ames, IA: Iowa State University Press, 1964).
11. Hirschman, A. O. *Development Projects Observed*, The Brookings Institution, Washington, DC (1967).

12. Bruton, H. J. *Principles of Development Economics* (Englewood Cliffs, NJ: Prentice-Hall, Inc., 1965).
13. Tinbergen, J. *The Design of Development* (Baltimore: The Johns Hopkins University Press, 1964).
14. Raj, K. N. *Some Economic Aspects of the Bhakra Nangal Project* (Bombay, India: Asia Publishing House, 1960).
15. "Proceedings of the Seventh Regional Conference on Water Resources Development in Asia and the Far East," United Nations Water Resources Series No. 32 (1967).
16. Vyas, V. S. "Some Aspects of Irrigation and Power Development," in *Foundations of Indian Agriculture*, V. Dagli, Ed. (Bombay, India: Vora & Company, 1968).
17. Myrdal, G. *Asian Drama* (New York: Pantheon Books, Inc., 1968).
18. Nair, K. *Blossoms in the Dust* (New York: Praeger Publishers, 1961).
19. Thorner, D., and A. Thorner. *Land and Labour in India* (Bombay, India: Asia Publishing House, 1962).
20. Gaitskell, A. "Problems of Policy in Planning the Indus Basin Investment in West Pakistan," in *Economic Development of Tropical Agriculture*, W. W. McPherson, Ed. (Gainesville, FL: University of Florida Press, 1968).

CHAPTER 7

SOME INSTITUTIONAL CONSTRAINTS
TO COASTAL ZONE MANAGEMENT:
A CASE STUDY OF HAWAII*

INTRODUCTION

The coastal zone plays a strategic role in the overwhelmingly marine economy of Hawaii. It is easily the state's most valuable marine asset. The general coastline of the Hawaiian Islands combined is 750 miles, the fourth largest among the states and territories, and equals almost half of the total open sea shoreline of the 48 contiguous states. It embraces the entirety of Hawaii's maritime activities, which account for over 95% of all the products aside from passengers moved to or from Hawaii or between the islands of the Hawaiian chain. The marine-related activities that occur in the state's coastal zone account for a broad spectrum of business-tourist services, boat building, marine construction, ship repair, brokerage agencies, warehousing, commercial diving and many more. The pressures of different uses on Hawaii's coastal zone have been mounting dramatically in recent years, causing an increasing variety of management problems.

This chapter is a first attempt to examine critically the factors which impede the formulation and implementation of an effective system for optimum management of Hawaii's vital shoreline. The problems that plague Hawaii's coastal zone

---

*Co-authored with Justin Rutka.

101

management are primarily the result of institutional factors, some of them rather unique. These are:

1. the oligopolistic structure of the state's shoreline ownership;
2. continuing conflicts and controversies among an array of shoreline interests: private owners, environmental and conservation groups, the government agencies;
3. jurisdictional overlapping and lack of interagency coordination; and
4. absence of effective institutional mechanisms to ascertain "public" interest and to incorporate it in coastal zone legislation.

SHORELINE OWNERSHIP: OLIGOPOLY IN ACTION

Hawaii has a unique pattern of land ownership that provides a clear example of oligopoly in action. Approximately 50% of the total land in Hawaii is owned by a few large private owners. (The corporations that own major portions of the Hawaiian coastline include: Bishop Estate, Castle and Cooke, Campbell Estate, Baldwin Packers, Dillingham, Damon Estate, and Gay and Robinson.) Large land holders own about 45% of the state's total shoreline and about 47% of its sandy shoreline. This, in effect, means that a major segment of the state's shoreline is owned and controlled by a handful of private corporations, which makes public access to a good portion of this area virtually impossible. Added to this is the fact that 20% of the coastal land owned by the government (federal and state), or about 7% of the total shoreline is earmarked for military use, and access by the public is either completely barred or considerably restricted—a fact of which the public is blissfully unaware. Thus, nearly 67% of the total shoreline and 75% of the sandy shoreline is owned between the military and private owners (Table I).

Table I. Oligopoly in Hawaii's Shoreline Ownership

| | Private | | | |
	Large Land Holdings (%)	Small Land Holdings (%)	Military (%)	Total (%)
Total Shoreline	45	15	7	67
Sandy Shoreline	47	19	9	75

It becomes clear from Table I that, on making allowance for legal impediments arising out of private and military ownership, only a small proportion of the state's coastline becomes available for public use. The "effective shoreline" (shoreline actually available for public use) is curtailed drastically, especially because of the legal constraints stemming from the oligopolistic nature of ownership. Add to this the fact that 50% of the shoreline is inaccessible to start with, because of physical characteristics. The effective shoreline then amounts to a mere 124 miles out of a total 750 miles, i.e., roughly 16%.

What follows is a discussion of some of the implications of corporate gigantism in the context of shoreline development. The most obvious result of this type of ownership is an erosion of considerably large areas of the shoreline from actual public use, although the beaches are a public resource and as such should always be available for public use. The public has been psychologically conditioned to view these as private property and a restructuring of perspectives and perceptions is hard to come by.

Another, perhaps a more serious, consequence is the type of development that has occurred on the Hawaiian shoreline in the last few decades. These have largely been dictated by considerations of profit maximization and have taken the form of urban, resort and residential developments. Although there is admittedly a need for development of this nature, the relevant question centers on the desirability of using prime shoreline areas to satisfy these demands, while alternative areas could be used for these purposes.

A third consequence is the emergence of a new breed of "landed aristocracy" that exerts a strong influence over some of the key decision-making bodies. There are several instances where decisions that favor the big corporations have been taken against the wishes of the citizenry. Finally, the compatibility of shoreline developments and activities to the larger overall developmental goals of the state and their impact on public welfare, environmental quality and the quality of life in general are often disregarded in arriving at decisions.

CONFLICT OF INTERESTS:
THE SWING OF THE PENDULUM

Hawaii's coastal zone development has been characterized by a large number of interest conflicts. For analytical purposes, the conflicts that have occurred in recent years could be classified into three categories:

1. conflicts between private developers and the conservation or environmental action groups;
2. conflicts between federal or state government and the public interest groups; and
3. occasionally, conflicts between the federal or state government and the private landowners.

The most vocal and acrimonious feuds have been between private developers and the conservation groups. A particularly revealing example pertains to the construction of a huge apartment complex in the rural Waianae shoreline of Oahu. The developers of the Makaha Surfside Condominium applied for rezoning to the Honolulu City Council that would permit them to build a 324-unit apartment complex on more than five acres of prime Waianae Coast beach property. The rezoning was opposed vigorously by the majority of local residents, the spokesmen of the Waianae Coast Model Cities Program and several other public interest groups on the grounds that it would deny the local people access to the beaches, besides completely ruining the beauty of the shoreline and disrupting the familiar, pressure-free lifestyle of the local residents. Despite strong protests, the City Council approved rezoning and the construction of the condominium. The council's action signaled a victory for the developers, stockholders and businessmen who supported the development on the ground that the project would bolster the economy of the area. By the same token, it suggested that the interests of the local residents were ignored completely. As Henry Peters, Director of the Waianae Resident Participation Organization, put it: "A majority of the Council ignored the many supporters of the park in favor of the few developers and speculators" [1].

Conflicts between government and environmental action groups can be illustrated in terms of the proposed construction of a $46 million, 12,500-foot offshore reef runway at the Honolulu International Airport. The State Department of Transportation, responsible for the construction of the reef runway, considers it "an outstanding example of a major public project to bring man and his environment into more productive harmony" [2]. This claim was challenged by several environmental groups, most notably Life of the Land. This group maintained that the environmental impact statement prepared by the state Department of Transportation failed to point out the adverse environmental effects of the reef runway project. Efforts were undertaken by the group to ensure a thorough review of the impact statement by the President's Council on Environmental Quality before the go-ahead was given to the project. The central issues surrounding the controversy were safety for airport area residents, noise and water pollution, and the cost involved.

Despite objections raised by Life of the Land and other environmental groups, the Federal Aviation Administration (FAA) and the U.S. Department of Transportation (DOT) gave approval to the project in May 1972. It was, of course, claimed that careful consideration was given to the objections. The last obstacle was removed when the U.S. Army Corps of Engineers was cleared by the U.S. Environmental Protection Agency (EPA) to okay the reef runway in July 1972.

The Life of the Land was quick to act, as was to be expected. It formed, in opposition to the engineers' position, a Coalition for Airport Alternatives that included KOKUA Hawaii, Save Our Surf and other ecology action groups. These groups filed a suit seeking an injunction against the construction of the reef runway. However, this request was denied by the court in December 1972. The state has now signed a $46 million contract with the Dillingham Corporation for major work on the construction of the reef runway.

The Life of the Land, however, seems to be unrelenting in its efforts to halt the project. In a surprise move, the ecology group issued a statement that it has marshaled new evidence pertaining to air pollution, and that it has received permission (from the federal judge) to renew its suit seeking a permanent injunction against the project.

The continuing struggle between the groups provides a fascinating illustration of the classic confrontation between economics and ecology that seems to occur with an almost alarming frequency in the critical coastal landscapes of the nation as a whole.

An example of conflict between government and private landowners is provided by the 1969 Honolulu City Council ordinance which designated residential land in the exclusive Diamond Head Terrace area for public park use that allows land acquisition for the construction of a public park along the shoreline. A number of owners opposed this. The homeowners contended that the City Council had not fulfilled all the necessary steps to permit the city to change its General Plan. The area had been zoned for residential and apartment use in the General Plan and the 1969 ordinance changed the General Plan. switched 29.29 acres of residence and 6.8 acres of apartment land to park use. However, the legality of the ordinance was upheld in a court ruling.

JURISDICTIONAL OVERLAPPING:
THE SHADOWY LANDSCAPE

There is a good deal of jurisdictional overlapping and lack of interagency coordination in the planning and management of Hawaii's coastal areas. No clear-cut delineation of functions has been made among the various federal, state and county agencies that have jurisdiction. The prevailing zoning regulations and land use law of the state to a certain extent reflect this functional overlapping.

Closely related to and stemming from jurisdictional overlapping is the problem of lack of coordination among the various agencies which have a stake in this vital environment. As the report on "Hawaii and the Sea" points out:

> . . . various responsibilities for each of its (the coastal zone's) facets were fractionated among federal, state, county, and military entities in Hawaii. As a result of this overly broad dissemination of responsibilities, there is no individual agency that can establish policy and delegate authority in dealing with problems ranging from water pollution to beach sand removal. . . [3].

An especially striking example of overlapping jurisdiction is provided by the State Department of Transportation, which has plenary responsibility as well as authority for managing the shoreline. However, the Department of Transportation's "commercial orientation" has often generated conflicts with recreation agencies for the shoreline. An instance in point is Sand Island, which the state recently obtained as surplus land from the federal government. The Department of Transportation wants to use the land for expansion of harbor facilities and related activities. The Division of State Parks would like to develop a beach park there to meet the rapidly growing recreational demands of Honolulu's residents. In the absence of an overall policy on shoreline uses, resolution of conflicts among different agencies often tends to be an exercise in futility.

Another instance in point is the State Land Use Law, which vests the state and county governments with control over the use of land. However, the Department of Transportation has concurrent jurisdiction over the use of the shore and submerged lands. Because there is no overriding policy on which to base decisions, a project approved by one body could very well be disapproved by another. The State Comprehensive Recreation Plan noted:

> Likewise, the Department of Land and Natural Resources determines the specific uses for which state lands, including submerged lands, can be leased. Transportation Department can overrule Department of Land and Natural Resource's determination of a shore use. The state's use and development of its submerged land and the shoreline is subject to review and approval by the U.S. Corps of Engineers for navigational and flood control concerns. Again, conflicts can arise over proposed use because of a lack of clear policy [4].

The other examples that further illustrate the situation are: the State Department of Health has power to close beaches without consulting other agencies when a health hazard is determined; state-county disputes occur about who should clean up the beaches; and disagreements exist between state and county over who should run the parks.

PUBLIC INTEREST:
THE FORGOTTEN DIMENSION

A survey of the various developments that have occurred in Hawaii's coastal zone over the past several years leads to the conclusion that they have not always been dictated by considerations of public interest. In fact, there is ample evidence to suggest that public interest in many cases has been completely overlooked in making decisions that have a profound and pronounced bearing on the lives of the people.

For the purposes of this chapter, the term "public interest" is defined as referring to "A general aggregate denoting what is on balance good for the citizenry" [5]. As Lindblom points out, "The pursuit of the public interest, general welfare or common good, is, then a comprehensive consideration in public policy making; and these terms refer to the most general and supreme goal of public policy" [5].

Feasible mechanisms to articulate and incorporate public interest have been all but absent in the generally somnolent Hawaiian setting. Specifically, the following reasons can be identified: (1) lack of concerned and informed leadership; (2) lack of public awareness because of limited exposure and publicity; (3) lack of funds and facilities to articulate public interest; (4) delaying tactics used by vested interests; and (5) sheer public apathy.

Two specific instances to substantiate what has been said above are cited below. Both are of recent origin, suggesting that there has been no perceptible change in the decision-making process. First, several meetings were held in 1972 by the Sunset Beach Community Association to voice opposition to the development of an amusement park in the middle of the wildly beautiful Kahuku area. Opportunities were provided to the local businessmen, the developers and the Bishop Estate to express their viewpoints, of which they did not make use. The end result: The Honolulu City Council chose to ignore community feelings, and gave the go-ahead to the massive resort development. Second, the Department of Defense undertook in 1972 a detailed study on military land-use in Hawaii. The study team from Washington, DC which spent several days in Hawaii, refused to make provisions for public hearings, although written testimony from groups and individuals was accepted. What is more, even the City Council was not provided an opportunity to make its views heard. Information from the city is needed partly because the city may save millions for future parks if much military land reverts to public use. (The military owns outright or leases about 28% of all the land on Oahu.) A sizable part of the military land happens to be within the coastal zone.

There are, however, strong indications that the long-emasculated public is at last making concerted efforts to re-assert itself. A major effort in this direction is symbolized by the Hui Malama, a new citizens' group formed to preserve the traditional lifestyles of the Hawaiians against the onslaught of developers. Its opposition is directed specifically at a proposed rezoning of rural Kahuluu to an apartment and residence area. This will transform the rural Kahuluu community that nestles in the shoreline into a suburb for the wealthy. (Such a situation occurred in the Kalama Valley, where rural Hawaiians were displaced from Bishop Estate land to make room for Hawaii Kai suburban development.) Hui Malama does not want to block development totally, but wants to participate constructively in shaping the plans. It stands for "Development that builds on the life of the people, that preserves our values, and that nourishes the children and grandchildren of all local people of Hawaii" [6].

CONCLUSIONS

It should be clear from the above discussion that institutional impediments have considerably slowed the balanced development and optimum use of Hawaii's vital shoreline areas. Concentration of corporate and military ownership has made a significant proportion of Hawaii's coastal zone inaccessible to the public. A disquieting array of interest conflicts has always plagued the state's shoreline development. Jurisdictional overlapping and the consequent lack of coordination have posed formidable difficulties in shoreline management. And to top it all, almost complete disregard for public interest has made even the fragmentary efforts at coastal zone planning at best an exercise in futility. Thus, institutional factors, despite their overriding importance, have received scant attention in formulating the state's coastal zone policy. Viewed against this bleak background, the need for drastically revamping Hawaii's archaic institutional infrastructure in delineating a sound and efficient strategy, becomes readily apparent.

REFERENCES

1. *The Honolulu Star Bulletin* (December 8, 1971), p. A-14.
2. Wright, E. A. Speech reported in *The Honolulu Advertiser* (April 12, 1972) p. A-3.
3. "Hawaii and the Sea" (Honolulu, HI: Department of Planning and Economic Development, State of Hawaii, 1969), p. 95.
4. "State Comprehensive Recreation Plan" (Honolulu, HI: Department of Planning and Economic Development, State of Hawaii, 1971), pp. 101–102.
5. Lindblom, C. *The Intelligence of Democracy* (New York: The Free Press, 1965), p. 275.
6. *The Honolulu Star Bulletin* (April 27, 1972) p. B-1.

CHAPTER 8

COASTAL ZONE USE CONFLICTS
AND THEIR IDENTIFICATION:
THE USE OF COMPATIBILITY MATRIXES

INTRODUCTION

The variety and intensity of uses in the Hawaiian coastal zone have increased dramatically in recent years. This spectacular growth has led to a disquieting array of use and interest conflicts that have stymied the optimum use of the scarce coastal zone resources and has adversely affected public interest.

This chapter attempts to study some of Hawaii's coastal zone conflicts, examines their impact on public interest and suggests a technique for the identification of use conflicts. The chapter first identifies, describes and discusses a number of use conflicts that have resulted from the development of Hawaii's coastal zone for recreational (resort), urban and industrial purposes. This is followed by an appraisal of the impact of these conflicts on public needs and public interest. The chapter concludes with a discussion of "compatibility matrixes" and their application to conflict identification in the context of shoreline development.

113

SHORELINE DEVELOPMENT
AND USE CONFLICTS

A scrutiny of the pattern of Hawaii's shoreline development suggests that it has occurred in a manner best suited to private interests or special interest groups, and that considerations of public interest have often been relegated to the background. This is, in fact, a logical outcome of the special set of circumstances surrounding ownership of the Hawaiian shoreline, and is also the result of the absence of specific regulatory mechanisms for charting the course of the state's shoreline development with a view to safeguarding public interest. Jurisdictional overlapping resulting from a lack of clear-cut delineation of functions among the various agencies concerned with shoreline management has further contributed to the difficulty. In sum, there simply doesn't exist a body of well-defined criteria or guidelines to ensure the effective allocation of Hawaii's vital shoreline resources.

The most striking and visible result of the unplanned development of the Hawaiian coastal zone has been the emergence of a disquieting array of use conflicts. For analytical purposes, these conflicts can be classified into two categories: (1) conflicts arising from massive resort development by private developers; and (2) conflicts arising from coastal water pollution from rapid urbanization and industrialization.

The most frequent conflicts have been between resort developers and the local residents. Waikiki offers a particularly revealing example of this kind of conflict. For all intents and purposes, the Waikiki beaches are "lost to the local residents," because entry to the beaches is exclusively reserved for hotel guests by the huge hotels fronting them. In most instances, there is no provision for public right-of-way to the beaches.

What is true of Waikiki is in large measure true of resort areas on outer islands. The Poipu Beach resort hotels on Kauai and the Kaanapali resort complex on Maui are instances in point. The situation is probably worse on the Big Island of Hawaii, where beaches are few and far between, and the private hotels fronting them adhere strictly to their policy of denying entry to the beaches to the local people.

The parties to the conflict are the private developers on the one hand, and the local residents on the other. What is at stake is the inalienable right of the people to enjoy their beaches. The central issue is public access.

Another conflict situation resulting from massive resort and recreational development is exemplified by the Kuhio Beach widening controversy. The U.S. Army Corps of Engineers wanted to widen the Kuhio Beach located in the center of Waikiki to accommodate more people. (The beach is almost exclusively used by out-of-state tourists residing in the hotels fronting this beach.) This was strongly opposed by environmental groups, especially Save Our Surf (SOS), on the grounds that beach-widening would destroy several excellent surfing sites used extensively by the local residents and damage irreparably the surrounding marine environment. The environmental impact statement prepared by the Corps pointed out that no damage to the marine environment would result from the proposed action. This was challenged by Save Our Surf. The controversy between the two groups raged for a long time, and the two parties finally worked out a compromise formula that allowed widening, but on a reduced scale.

The parties to the conflict were on the one hand, the Army Corps of Engineers who, in the public eye, represented the interests of the hotel owners, and the environmental groups, who came to be regarded as the spokesmen of the local public. At stake were the interests of the local surfing enthusiasts, who stood to lose from the destruction of the surfing sites.

Other conflicts unleashed by the runaway development of resort hotels are: visual pollution from the massive array of skyscrapers lining the beach front, obscuring the view of Diamond Head and other aesthetically pleasing shoreline vistas; "people pollution" from overcrowding and congestion on the beaches; and noise pollution from incessant construction activity that plagues the shoreline areas.

The second set of conflicts arises from rapid urbanization and industrialization encompassing residential, commercial and industrial activities. These activities have been contributing substantially to coastal water pollution during the past several years.

With increasing urbanization and increasing population density in the urban areas, cesspool disposal of sewage has given way to sanitary sewer systems that discharge into the ocean. Such systems carry industrial wastes, especially wastes from the pineapple canneries, as well as domestic wastes. Most of these systems have no sewage treatment facilities, so raw sewage is discharged into the sea. As a result of this, the supply of *nehu*, the most important baitfish for tuna fishing, has declined markedly, and more than 35 million oysters in the west loch section of Pearl Harbor were recently polluted by animal waste and the untreated sewage system near the loch.

Choice recreational areas are being made unfit for recreational activities because of unregulated waste disposal practices. A classic case of such abuse is that of Kaneohe Bay, on Oahu, an ideal recreational area for boating, fishing and water contact sports. Waste discharges into the bay have resulted in "coral kill, disappearance of clams, overgrowth of green-bubble algae, and increases in the phosphorus and nitrogen in Bay waters" [1].

The enormous discharge of sugarmill wastes has resulted in significant increases in the turbidity of coastal waters, primarily from soil and bagasse. The growth of marine organisms has been adversely affected, although the extent of this has not been fully determined. The trash constitutes a hazard to navigation and leads to stagnation problems in some harbors.

The conflicts between the parties involved provide a fascinating illustration of the classic confrontation between economics and ecology that seems to be occurring with an almost alarming frequency in the critical coastal landscapes of the nation as a whole.

IMPACT ON PUBLIC INTEREST

It should be clear from the foregoing discussion that the use conflicts have been essentially the result of competing demands on the limited resources of the coastal zone. Although some of the conflicts are the result of the basic incompatibility of uses, others stem from the nature of ownership of the coastal zone.

In many instances, private pursuit of profit is at the expense of public interest, a situation where the market forces of supply and demand are an imperfect guide to equitable decision-making. As Mishan puts it, "The net gains of the fortune-seekers themselves, however, is of less concern to us than the effects on the public at large" [2]. Thus, even when purely economic considerations dictate further expansion of resort development in prime shoreline areas, considerations of public interest such as access and environmental quality might dictate a different course of action. However, in the absence of regulatory mechanisms or institutional arrangements to resolve use conflicts, public interest is bound to suffer. Nevertheless, there is growing evidence of these conflicts coming to a head. Mishan, in this connection, draws pointed attention to the "conflict between those enterprises that for years have been pouring their waste products into the once-fresh waters of lakes and rivers and the public at large, a fact of life that is belatedly being discovered by journalists and by citizens who are being deprived of the use of such waters for drinking, fishing, or bathing" [2].

The term "public interest" is defined in this context as referring to "A general aggregate denoting what is on balance good for the citizenry" [3]. As Lindblom points out, "The pursuit of the public interest, general welfare or common good, is, then a comprehensive consideration in public policy making; and these terms refer to the most general and supreme goal of public policy" [3].

Corporate ownership of large segments of the coastal zone has the following implications for public interest. First, it leads to erosion of considerably large areas of the shoreline from actual public use, although the beaches are a public resource, and as such should always be available for public use. The public has been psychologically conditioned to view these as private property, and a restructuring of perspectives and perceptions is hard to come by. Another consequence, and perhaps a more serious one, is the type of development that has occurred in Hawaii's shoreline in the last few decades. These have been largely dictated by considerations of profit maximization. Although there is admittedly a need for developments of this nature, the relevant question centers on the desirability of using prime shoreline areas to satisfy these demands, when alternative areas could be used for these purposes. Finally, the compatibility of shoreline developments and activities to the larger overall developmental goals of the state and their impact on public welfare, environmental quality and the quality of life in general is often disregarded in arriving at decisions.

IDENTIFYING USE CONFLICTS: THE USE OF COMPATIBILITY MATRIXES

As the intensity of coastal zone use conflicts increases, the need to develop effective techniques to identify such conflicts is bound to become progressively pressing. An attempt is made in this section to demonstrate the use of one such technique. This technique involves the use of "compatibility matrixes."

The compatibility matrix enables a planner to assess the impact of a proposed or planned use on existing uses. It helps him to ascertain whether a proposed use is highly compatible, moderately compatible, poorly compatible or incompatible with one or several existing uses. The application of this technique is explored here in terms of two types of compatibility matrixes.

The first matrix (Figure 1) shows the degree of compatibility among 24 coastal zone uses and activities. The interrelationship between the different uses is expressed in terms of five categories, defined as follows:

1. *essential* coastal zone uses or activities essential to orderly coastal and offshore development;
2. *supplemental* coastal zone uses that eventually tend to supplement one another economically without conflict;

3. *mutually exclusive*: only one such coastal use can be accomplished to the exclusion of all others;
4. *competitive* activities that can go on simultaneously but between which there will always be argument for priority, political favor of position, legal precedence, etc.; and
5. *indeterminant*: no discernible relationship; at least none of any consequence [4].

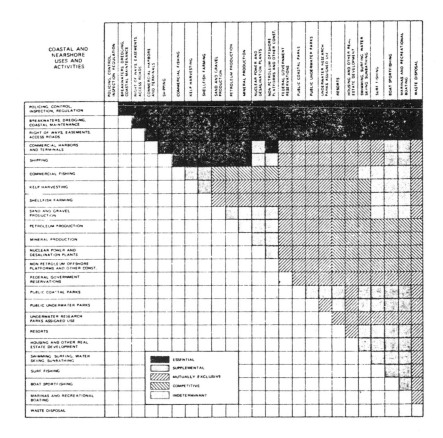

Figure 1. Compatibility matrix: coastal and nearshore uses and activities (source: Dr. Gordon Lill).

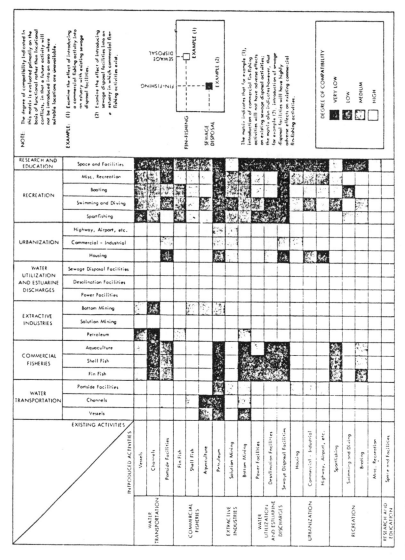

Figure 2. Matrix of degree to which an introduced activity is compatible with an existing estuarine use (source: Wilsey & Ham and U.S. Department of Interior).

The matrix shows that right-of-way easements or access roads are essential to resort development. Similarly, it becomes clear from this matrix that commercial fishing is supplemental to kelp harvesting and shellfish farming; mutually exclusive of public coastal and underwater parks; competitive with sand and gravel production, petroleum production, mineral production and waste disposal; and its effect on activities such as swimming, surfing, water-skiing or surf fishing is indeterminant. Thus, with the aid of this matrix, it is possible to scrutinize the impact of an activity or use on an array of other activities or uses, and on the basis of the information gathered to chart the course for optimum resource allocation.

The second matrix (Figure 2) shows the degree to which an introduced activity is compatible with an existing coastal zone use [5]. For example, it can be seen from the matrix that the introduction of commercial fin-fishing activities will not have harmful effects on existing sewage disposal facilities. However, the matrix also shows that the introduction of sewage disposal facilities will have highly deleterious consequences on existing commercial fin-fishing activities.

The use of compatibility matrixes as part of a detailed resource capability analysis should aid coastal zone planners considerably in allocating the scarce coastal zone resources in an optimal fashion. The matrixes could serve as much-needed guides or pointers to steer clear of potential use conflicts and the consequent waste of precious resources.

REFERENCES

1. Dugan, G. L., and H. F. Young. "Coastal Waste Disposal Practices in Hawaii," *Quality of Coastal Waters Project Bulletin,* Sea Grant Program, WRRC, University of Hawaii, p.2.
2. Mishan, E. J., *The Costs of Economic Growth* (New York: Praeger Publishers, 1967).
3. Lindblom, C. *The Intelligence of Democracy* (New York: The Free Press, 1965), p. 275
4. J. F. Peel Brahtz, Ed. *Coastal Zone Management: Multiple Use with Conservation,* (New York: John Wiley & Sons, 1972), pp. 166–167.
5. Wenk, E., Jr. *The Politics of the Ocean,* (Seattle, WA: The University of Washington Press, 1972), p. 179.

CHAPTER 9

ECONOMIC POTENTIAL OF BAGASSE
AS AN ALTERNATIVE ENERGY SOURCE:
THE HAWAIIAN EXPERIENCE*

INTRODUCTION

The progressive escalation of energy shortages in recent years
has led to an intensified search for feasible alternative sources
of energy in virtually every part of the United States. This is
especially true of Hawaii, whose economic and geographic characteristics have constrained its present source of supply to a
single fossil fuel: oil. This monopoly of oil is further enhanced
by the crucial role of transportation in the economic life of the
islands dominated by tourism, plantation agriculture and military services. Viewed in this perspective, the need for exploring
and exploiting alternative sources of energy in the Hawaiian
islands becomes urgent and compelling.

Alternative energy sources such as geothermal, ocean thermal, solar, wind and silviculture appear to be promising in
Hawaii from a geographic, environmental and renewable-
resource perspective. However, there are several technical and
socioeconomic uncertainties involved in their use [1]. Their
long-run feasibility, nevertheless, is an important aspect of
Hawaiian energy research and development efforts, but their
immediate application on a commercial-scale is of a limited
nature. Therefore, a renewable energy source is needed whose
utilization system is presently operational and amenable to

---

*Co-authored with Michael Nahan.

expansion. Such a source in Hawaii is bagasse, the fibrous residue of sugarcane left after crushing and extraction of the juices.

This chapter examines four basic strategies for large-scale production of electricity using bagasse as fuel; describes the extent to which the sugar industry in Hawaii has progressed in this respect to date; estimates the potential generating capacity of the industry; and proposes some specific measures for optimizing the use of bagasse.

INSTITUTIONAL SETTING

The Hawaiian sugar industry consists of 18 plantations that control or lease 240,000 acres plus an additional 17,500 acres controlled by independent growers. The sugarmills are located along the coastlines of the four sugar islands (Figure 1). These plantations are owned and operated by five Hawaii-based companies (known as factors), which in recent years have diversified away from their local agricultural base. The research, final refining and marketing are done on an industry-wide, cooperative basis through the Hawaiian Sugar Planters' Association and the C & H Refineries in California [2].

The industry is the third largest in the state, and plays an especially important role in the economies of the islands of Maui, Kauai and Hawaii (Table I). The energy needs of these three islands are largely accounted for by the industrial, residential and tourist sectors. These three islands will have the greatest potential for utilization of bagasse as a fuel source. Oahu, the other sugar-producing island, has 60% of the state's population and plantations that are very energy-intensive because of high irrigation demands; thus the potential contribution of bagasse to the total energy needs of this island is minimal.

The industry has shown a good deal of adaptability and ingenuity in response to numerous seemingly formidable constraints. For example, the industry's high capital-intensity is attributable to the very high cost of agricultural labor. Vigorous

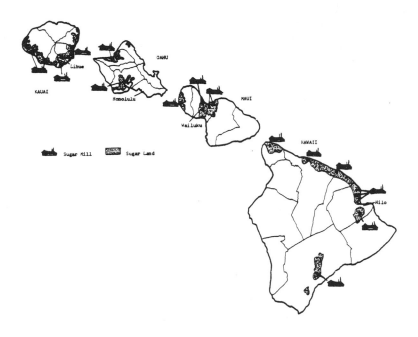

Figure 1. Hawaii's sugar islands [2].

Table I. Sugarcane Acreage and Sugar Production in Hawaii, 1974 [2]

Island	Cane Acreage	Raw Sugar (tons)
Hawaii	98,744	390,000
Kauai	45,721	227,242
Maui	46,250	259,606
Oahu	33,512	163,894
Total	224,227	1,040,742

and sustained efforts to maximize the yields of sugar and sugar-cane per acre reflect the industry's resolve to make up for the relatively stagnant sugar prices.

Although the industry is durable and profitable, numerous factors are presently contributing to the uncertainties within the industry. The Sugar Act, which regulated prices and markets for 25 years, expired in December 1974, leaving a void. This left the U.S. market open to unregulated competition from foreign, state-controlled or subsidized sugar companies. Although new sugar legislation may be introduced when world prices stabilize, present conditions are not conducive to long-range planning. Recent advances in corn-based sweetener have made significant inroads into the natural sugar market. The opportunity cost of some prime agricultural lands is increasing because of demands of residential and industrial growth. These uncertainties are major considerations in assessing the investment behavior and production practices for maximizing electricity generation from bagasse.

BAGASSE AS AN ENERGY SOURCE

The sugar industry can become a significant supplier of electrical power to the island's utility grid through four basic strategies:

1. expansion of generating capacity;
2. expansion of the quantity of bagasse;
3. improvement in the quality of bagasse; and
4. reduction of the sugar industry's electrical consumption.

Expansion of Generating Capacity

The original steam and generating facilities at all mills are composed of boilers using bagasse that operate at a pressure of about 150 psi. For maximum consumption of bagasse, high-pressure boilers at 400–850 psi must be used in conjunction with extraction condensing turbine generators. This can only be justified when existing boilers need replacing. Two plantations on Hawaii, two on Maui and one on Kauai have expanded in this manner, with numerous plantations presently or in the near future requiring replacement. The existing boilers can use fuel oil, bagasse or a mixture of both. When bagasse is in short supply, or has high moisture content, fuel oil can be used.

Expansion of the Quantity of Bagasse

Until the energy crisis, bagasse was considered a waste product because of its inability to compete with oil as a fuel and also because of its by-product relationship to sugar. Therefore, the only consideration pertaining to the supply of fibrous matter has been its reduction. To expand the supply of bagasse, a reversal of this mode of thinking must be brought about in the industry, and concomitant technical means must be explored to expand the quantity of fibrous matter.

Fibrous matter, which is a primary concern in analyzing the fuel qualities of bagasse, is produced in an amount that is approximately fixed in proportion to the output of sugar, given optimum sugar-yield conditions. Quantities of fibrous matter can be introduced into the selection of material or cane variety. The amount of fibrous matter can be increased by stopping the practice of preharvest burning, although this has led in the past to a congestion problem at the mill.

A unique problem facing the Hawaiian sugar industry is the marked variation in terrain that it experiences within a small area. This has resulted in specialized harvesting equipment and techniques. The use of V-cutters, push rakes and cranes, rather than mechanical harvesters, results in large amounts of fibrous matter remaining in the fields and large amounts of dust and extraneous matter in the harvested cane. The design of a mechanical harvester to suit the rather pronounced variation in slope has been and is a primary research goal. Numerous plantations have successfully introduced a model, and its range of application is presently being ascertained [3].

Quality Improvement

The primary yardstick of bagasse quality is its moisture content. The moisture content can be reduced by means of the bagasse dryer, which uses stack exhaust to dry the bagasse. Dryers not only decrease the moisture content but also decrease the need for fuel oil and increase the efficiency of the boilers [4]. The diffusion milling system is another method that results in lower moisture content, and also reduced use of electricity. The introduction of the diffusion process is only possible as old crushers approach obsolescence. Introduction of a pneumatic cleaning system in place of the water system can potentially decrease the moisture content of the cane as well as the water use of the mill.

A major consideration in the commercial use of bagasse as a fuel is the storage of bagasse for generation during the nonharvest period. Numerous forms have been researched, e.g., pellets, briquettes, baled and depithed. All of these have the combined characteristics of higher fiber content, lower moisture, more compactness and greater stability of state than unprocessed bagasse [5].

Reduction of Consumption

The high rate of electricity consumption of the sugar industries, which ranges from 30 to 90% of the three sugar islands' total electrical consumption, is caused by the former need to dispose of waste bagasse [1]. Now that the price of oil has quadrupled and the Environmental Protection Agency (EPA) has levied large fines against alternative forms of bagasse disposal, the plantations have begun to reconsider their current consumption patterns. The major use of electricity is for irrigation, the incidence of which varies with climatic conditions, resulting in large variations in plantation consumption. The most significant breakthrough in irrigation technology has been drip irrigation, which not only decreases the use of electricity and water by about 50%, but also allows for the introduction of previously marginal lands to cane production [6]. Another method to curtail electrical consumption is to effect changes in the consumption pattern with a view to eliminate waste. Also, diffusion milling equipment and multieffect evaporators can decrease energy consumption [6].

THE HAWAIIAN EXPERIENCE

Bagasse has been used by the island sugar industry as a fuel source since its inception 100 years ago. The industry today is an established medium of considerable size and adaptability that has extensive generating capacity.

Plantations on the windward side of the islands, where irrigation requirements are minor, have always had an excess supply of bagasse. Since 1969, in response to EPA requirements, numerous plantations have enlarged their boiler capacity as a means of bagasse disposal. In doing so, they entered into contractual arrangements with the utilities to supply electricity at a fixed rate. On Hawaii, 22,000 kW supplied to the Hawaiian Electric Company (HECO) accounted for 30% of the island's electricity demand, excluding the plantations' use. On Kauai, 28% of the island's demand, exclusive of plantation needs, was met by plantation sales to the utilities [7]. On the islands of Maui and Oahu, because of irrigation requirements, the plantations maintain a demand-supply equilibrium with respect to the utilities. Figure 2 shows current plantation sales to the utilities, possible additions to plantation sales through the use of drip irrigation and dryers, and the sales theoretically realizable on the islands of Hawaii, Kauai and Maui, and for the state as a whole.

The sugar industry has a long-established, two-way distribution system with the utilities to supply a fixed amount. The contractual arrangements established by the plantations that presently supply electricity to the utilities on a fixed basis are adequate for use under expanded conditions. The utility agrees to purchase a fixed amount of electricity from the firm and to pay the fixed cost for the generating capacity needed to

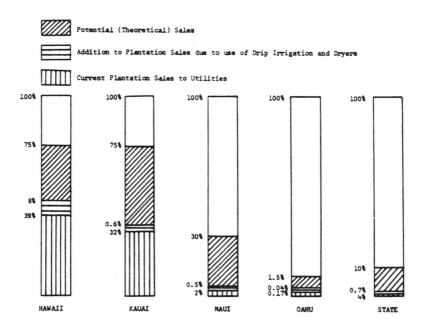

Figure 2. 1974 and potential sugar plantation sales to public utilities.

produce this amount. The rate is set by the utility's generating cost and price of oil, not including hydroelectric. The cost of expanding the transmission system would have to be subject to negotiations.

The utilities have offered a significant profit margin via the present contractual agreements. Hilo Coast Processing Company presently supplies 20% of the island of Hawaii's total electricity demand [8]. The cost of additional capacity of the plantation is being paid by the utility at $360,000/yr. It is estimated that with efficient production of bagasse, $2 million profit can be made from electrical generators alone. Present operational problems, e.g., cane dryers, new boilers and the diffusion system, have caused an irregular supply of bagasse, resulting in 55% use of fuel oil, negating any profit achieved through bagasse. The people involved maintain that all the operational difficulties will be ironed out, which would result in the stated $2 million profit. The successful results of Hilo Coast have spurred active interest in comparable arrangements.

The environmental impact of bagasse as a fuel source compared to wind, hydroelectric and ocean thermal power is shown in Table II. The table ranks each source in terms of a variety of environmental quality indicators using an impact severity rating system ranging from 1 to 4. The table shows that the environmental impact of bagasse is comparable to or less than that of other sources.

Table II. Evaluation of Environmental Impact of Alternative Energy Sources [1]

Impact	Severity Rating[a]			
	Bagasse	Wind	Hydro-electric	Ocean Thermal
Energy Resource Depletion	1	1	1	2
Area Committed for Conversion	1	3	3	3
Area Committed for Transmission	1	2	2	3
Water Consumption	1	1	1	3
Use of Airspace	1	3	1	1
Air Pollution	1	1	1	1
Water Pollution	1	1	1	2
Construction Activities	3	2	3	3
Heavy Metals or Toxic Substances	1	2	1	1
Thermal Discharge	3	1	1	2
Solid Waste	2	1	1	1
Visual Intrusion	1	4	2	1
Noise Generation	1	2	1	1
Public Health	1	1	1	2
Transportation Hazard	1	1	1	2

[a]Impact severity rating: 1 = negligible; 2 = slight; 3 = moderate; 4 = severe.

OPTIMIZING BAGASSE USE

This section attempts to identify and discuss some specific methods to optimize the use of bagasse. What follows is only a preliminary discussion, since a more sophisticated analysis is beyond the scope of this chapter.

The most difficult factor to analyze at this level of aggregation is the power plant. Each power plant is different with respect to age, components, plantation size, etc. For example, on Hawaii it would theoretically be possible to generate about 58,000 kW in addition to present generation if steam pressure were 400 psi, or about 75,000 kW if steam pressure were 850 psi, provided the following two conditions are met: installation of new high-pressure boilers of adequate size to use all of the bagasse and leafy trash, and installation of extraction condensing turbine generators of suitable size at each mill, with extracted steam furnishing the entire 150-psi steam requirements [7]. This includes no fuel use or off-season supply of electricity through use of bagasse. For a total electrical demand on the island of Hawaii of (100,000 kW), this would mean that the theoretical potential is 75% of the present demand [9]. Similar situations are apparent on Maui and Kauai. However, Oahu, with 60% of the state's population and heavily irrigated plantations, has a relatively minor potential for bagasse use.

Choice of boiler size depends mostly on the estimated supply of bagasse. In the analysis of the optimum boiler capacity, the primary consideration is the estimation of the supply, quality of bagasse and the associated characteristics of the present milling equipment which require the investigation of the potential bagasse expansion techniques. Two estimates are given below. The variability of the factors involved for the aggregate industry would decrease the reliability of these theoretical estimates.

1. Cane drying by use of stack gas is being investigated by all plantations and is of major significance [10, 11]. According to one estimate, its introduction can increase generating ability by 10%, with existing capacity.
2. Drip irrigation has resulted in a marked increase in cane (fibrous matter) and sugar yield, and a 30% improvement in water use efficiency compared to flume and overhead irrigation. This can result in a

maximum increase in electrical supply of 10% on Kauai and Hawaii and 15% on Maui and Oahu [2, 3,12].

The other methods to expand the bagasse supply are of minor short-run significance because of problems in meshing with existing technology, unwarranted capital costs and a lack of research on the potential value of increasing the production of bagasse.

The theoretical generating capacity of the sugar industry on Hawaii and Kauai is 75% of the present demand on these islands [7]. Although this theoretical capacity is questionable, significant potential obviously exists. This capacity can be optimally approached by changing the industry's concept of bagasse from that of a waste to one of a profitable product.

CONCLUSIONS

It is clear from the above discussion that the economic potential of bagasse as an alternative energy source for Hawaii is promising. Bagasse has been used by the island sugar industry for over 100 years, thus enabling it to fulfill the necessary conditions for user on a commercial scale [13]. The capital requirements of large-scale bagasse use are minor compared to those of other energy sources. Its impact on the environment is relatively insignificant. It is a renewable resource whose production does not require the extensive use of any scarce material.

This study shows that bagasse could meet a significant part of the energy needs of the islands of Hawaii, Kauai and Maui. However, its impact on Oahu, the major population center of the state, is minimal.

Ultimate realization of the theoretical potential of bagasse as an alternate energy source would depend on a number of technical, economic and institutional factors identified and discussed briefly in this chapter. The most important single change needed is, perhaps, a reversal of the traditional thinking in industry which often tends to treat bagasse as an agricultural waste product rather than a vital energy source.

REFERENCES

1. "Alternate Energy Sources for Hawaii," Department of Planning and Economic Development and University of Hawaii, Honolulu, HI (1975).
2. "Sugar Manual," Hawaii Sugar Planters' Association, Honolulu, HI (1975).
3. Leffingwell, R. V. "Field Mechanization," *Sugar Azucar* 71(1):30–34 (1976).
4. Ken, E. W. "Waste Fuel Drying and the Energy Crisis," *Sugar J.* 37(10):40–48 (1975).
5. Paturau, J. M. *By Products of the Cane Sugar Industry* (New York: Elsevier Publishing Company, 1969), pp. 43–58.
6. "Recent Developments in the Hawaiian Sugar Industry," *Sugar Azucar Yearbook 1969* 37:21–32 (1969).
7. "Bagasse Fuel Study for Hilo Electric Light Company," Bechtel Corporation, San Francisco, CA (1966).
8. First Hawaiian Bank. "Expanding Hawaii's Natural Energy," *Econ. Indicators* (November–December 1975), p. 1.
9. "Data Source Book," Department of Planning and Economic Development, Honolulu, HI (1975).
10. Bailliet, V. V. "Bagasse Drying Versus Air Pre-Heating," *Sugar J.* 38(10):52–53 (1976).
11. Hudson, V. C. "Sugarcane: Energy Relationship with Fossil Fuel," *Sugar J.* 38(5):25–28 (1975).
12. "Gilmore Louisiana, Florida, Hawaii Sugar Manual—1973," *Hawaiian Factory Index* 31:131–191 (1973).
13. Graham, R. W. "Fuels from Crops: Renewable and Clean," *Mech. Eng.* 97:27–31 (1975).

agricultural production   57,58,60, 77,83,86
agricultural system   60
Agriculture, Department of, U.S. (USDA)   60
agroclimatic zones   60
Amerasinghe, H.S.   40
ancillary energy   54,58,61
arid region   2,23
Arizona   24,29,32,35,73
Army Corps of Engineers   72,105, 108,115
Australia   39,42,43

bagasse   2,6,116,123,124,126-131
balance-of-payments   45
Ball, G.   46
Barlowe, R.   27
beneficial use   26
benefit-cost ratio   3,13,91
biomass   5
   See also bagasse
Brazil   42,43
Brewer, M.   17
Bruton, H. J.   90

California   17,24,29-32,36,50

California Correlative Doctrine   36
Canada   39,42,43
capital intensity   124
Central Valley Project   17
Chile   42,43
coastal water pollution   114,116
coastal zone
   conflict of interests   4,104-106,110,113
   jurisdictional overlapping   4, 107-110,114
   ownership   4,102-104,110,114
   right-of-way   114,121
   zoning regulations   107
   See also shoreline
Coffin v. Lefthand Ditch Company   29
Colorado   24,28,29,32
common property resources   40
"compatibility matrixes"   113, 118-121
conservancy districts   35,68-70
Criddle, W. D.   14

Defense, Department of   109
Desert Land Act, 1877   34

developed coastal states (DCS)
    42,43,45
Diamond Head 115
diffusion milling 128,129
drip irrigation 128,132
dynamics of change 7,97

economic development 12-14,16,
    96
economic energy 53,54,57,61
economic growth 1,3,13,15,75,86
economic zone 3,39-44
"effective shoreline" 103
embodied energy 54,58,61
employment potential 86-89
energy
    alternative sources 6,7,123
    budget 56,59
    flow models 5,51-53,55,61
    forms of energy 53,54,57,58,61
    inputs 50,51
    nonrenewable 57,58
    technology types 58,59
    units of measurement 58
    use coefficients 59
    See also ancillary energy;
        economic energy; embodied
        energy
Engineers, Corps of (U.S. Army)
    72,105,108,115
English doctrine 31
environmental action groups 105
environmental input 6,131,133
Environmental Protection Agency
    (EPA) 105,128,129
environmental quality 104,118
Environmental Quality, Council
    on 105
equity 21
externalities 15,19,20,45

Federal Aviation Administration
    (FAA) 105
federal participation 71
fisheries 41,43
flood control 69,81,82
fossil fuel 53,123

Gaitskell, A. 96
Galbraith, J. K. 46
Great Plains 25
green revolution 85,86,98

Hawaii 4-6,50,101-104,107-110,
    113,114,118,123-125,127,
    129,130,132,133
Hawaiian Electric Company
    (HECO) 129
Heichel 59
Hirschman, A. O. 92
holistic macroframework 2
horizontal transfers 17
hydropower 77,84,85,97
Huffman, R. 70
"Hui Malama" 110
Hutchins, W. A. 29,31,32

Idaho 24,31,32,71
India 2,3,39,42,75-79
    Five Year Plans 76,77
    Planning Commission 78
indirect benefits 3,90,91
Indonesia 42,43
inflationary cost-push 92
infrastructure 4,91
institutional constraints 76,92-97
institutional impediments 2,65,
    110
intermountain states 24

international waters   40
irrigation   77-82,85,86,88,89,92,
      94

Japan   39,40,42,43

Kaneohe Bay   116
Kansas   24,31,32
Kelso, M. M.   17,20
kilocalories (kcal)   58
Kindleberger, C.   46

labor-intensive projects   86,92
"landed aristocracy"   104
land use law   107
Las Vegas   35,36
Law of the Sea Conference   39
less-developed coastal states
      (LDCS)   3,4,42-45
Life of the Land   105,106
Lindblom, C.   109,117
liquefied petroleum gas (LPG)   54,
      57

Malagasy   42,43
manganese nodules   43
Mann, D. E.   35
marginal efficiency of capital   45
marine technology   4,43
Martin, R. C.   37
mechanization   88,89
Mexico   39,42-44
Montana   2,24,65-73
Montana Water Conservation Board
      67,70
multipurpose projects   15,67,69,
      77,86,89,97

Myrdal, G.   95
Mysore   94

Nagarjunasagar Dam   87
Nair, K.   93,94
National Water Resources Council
      72
Nevada   24,31,32,36,73
New Mexico   12,24,32,34,35,50,
      58
New Zealand   29,42,43
nonrenewable energy   57,58
North Dakota   24,31,68
Norway   42,43

ocean thermal energy   123,131
oil   39,43,44,123,130
Oklahoma   24,32,33
oligopoly   4,102,103
opportunity cost   126
Oregon   24,31,32,70,71

Pearl Harbor   116
"people pollution"   115
perspective plan   96
Philippines   39,42,43
politics of water   69
Portugal   42,43
preferential use   36
profit maximization   103,118
public access   115
public goods   18
public interest   4,104,108-110,
      113,114,116,117

quality of life
      104,118

Reclamation, Bureau of 20,72,73
Renne, R. R. 71
Renshaw, E. F. 14
resource allocation 5,40,114,121
riparian doctrine 24-26,29,32,36,
    37
Robinson, E. A. G. 84
Robinson, J. 73
rural electrification 77,82-85

Sarda Canal 94
Save Our Surf (SOS) 106,115
scientific manpower 43
secondary benefits 91
semiarid region 2,23
shoreline 4,101-103,105,110,113,
    114,118
silviculture 123
social costs 15
soil conservation 82,84
South Dakota 24,31,32
Soviet Union 42,43
stack gas 132
Stone, A. W. 67
sugar industry 124,133

Tannenbaum, F. 46
technology differential 62
Texas 24,31,35
Thompson, D. G. 31
Tinbergen, J. 90
Transportation, Department of
    (DOT) 105
Truman Proclamation 40
tubewells 80,83,85

United Nations Law of the Sea
    Conference, Third 39
U.S. Geological Survey 31
Utah 14,31,32
utilities 129,130
Uttar Pradesh 94

vertical transfers

Waikiki 114,115
water
    allocation among uses 2,11-
        14,16-20,66
    conservation 82
    ground water rights 30-36
    institutional aspects 65-74,
        92-97
    laws 23,37,66,67,95
    market for rights 16-19
    planning 89-92
    pricing 18-20
    surface water rights 28-30
    transfer 11-22
    underutilization 91,92
    value per acre-foot 14
    See also flood control; irri-
        gation; rural electrification
Water Commission Act of Cali-
    fornia 30
Webb, W. P. 25
welfare economics 20
wilderness areas 73
Wollman, N. 12
world ocean regime 47
world order models 46
Wyoming 15,24,28,29,31,32